Andrew Hirschl

The Law of Fraternities and Societies

With special Reference to their Insurance Feature

Andrew Hirschl

The Law of Fraternities and Societies
With special Reference to their Insurance Feature

ISBN/EAN: 9783337232832

Printed in Europe, USA, Canada, Australia, Japan

Cover: Foto ©Suzi / pixelio.de

More available books at **www.hansebooks.com**

OF

FRATERNITIES AND SOCIETIES.

A BOOK OF INTEREST TO MASONS, ODD FELLOWS, RED MEN,
DRUIDS, CHOSEN FRIENDS, FORESTERS, KNIGHTS OF
PYTHIAS, MEMBERS OF A. O. U. W., ROYAL ARCANUM,
K. OF H., L. OF H., AND OF ALL SIMILAR ORGANI-
ZATIONS, WITH SPECIAL REFERENCE TO
THEIR INSURANCE FEATURE.

BY A. J. HIRSCHL,
Of the Davenport (Iowa) Bar.

———————

ST. LOUIS, MO.:
WILLIAM H. STEVENSON,
LAW PUBLISHER AND PUBLISHER OF THE
CENTRAL LAW JOURNAL.
1883.

St. Louis, Mo.: Printed by the Central Law Journal.

TABLE OF CASES CITED.

THE LAW

OF

FRATERNITIES AND SOCIETIES.

---

§ 1. **Introductory Remarks.**— The object of the following pages is to bring into compact form cases decided in the courts of this country in relation to the various bodies named on the title page, and the effort was made to write in such a manner that the book can readily be understood by members of the societies, as indeed laymen in general, and for this reason the facts of the cases and extracts from the opinions are given, so that the matter may be fully comprehended by those who have not access to the law libraries. On the other hand, it is fair to suppose that these pages will not be entirely without interest or value to the lawyers. It is true that the cases given are, after all, but few, yet are they not for that very reason more difficult to find? Every practitioner knows that it is much easier to argue a case on promissory notes, for instance, where there are scores of decisions on every question, than it is to argue where there may be but one precedent, and that, perhaps, difficult to ascertain.

The topics considered are of great and increasing importance. The societies named on the title page include

(1)

over 1,500,000 members, and there are many others, such as Conductors' Associations, the Catholic Knights, etc., and as to their revenue, it is simply immense. The Odd Fellows alone are said to have an annual revenue of $5,000,000, counting the lower and higher bodies together. It must be borne in mind that nearly all of these societies issue insurance policies, thus aggregating, it may be said, hundreds of millions of dollars in risks and liabilities. Under these circumstances, it must be conceded that some information as to the rights and liabilities of members can not come amiss.

No one book thus far has covered the matters of interest, and it is safe to say that the purchaser of this book will find in it what would otherwise have to be laboriously searched for throughout the numerous volumes of a library; but there has been no attempt made to include the ordinary and well known rules concerning corporations; these must be found in the usual books.

Cases concerning building associations, religious bodies and boards of trade, are not included in this book, except a few by way of illustration, as there are now extant separate works on these subjects; neither are all cases given in which societies were involved; those which turned on the ordinary principles of contracts, evidence, etc., are omitted, and only those given in which the decision deals with some phase peculiar to these bodies. There are given, also, English decisions, and cases concerning irregularly organized bodies, e. g., political committees, etc., which cases tend to illustrate the topics in hand.

But it may be stated right here that cases involving associations organized with a view to pecuniary profit, have been studiously omitted, it being deemed that such are neither decisive, nor even illustrative, of the rights and liabilities of members of the bodies under consideration, although in several text books, and indeed in many cases, decided by able judges at that, these two different kinds of associations may be found referred to, respectively, as though they occupied the same position.

The limited scope of this work has made any extensive
plan of chapters, divisions and subdivisions unnecessary,
but the Index will be found to be very comprehensive.

THE NATURE OF THESE BODIES.

Evidently if the nature of the bodies under discussion is
once fairly understood, many other topics can be the more
easily disposed of.

§ 2. **Are they Co-Partnerships?**— While it has been said,
or rather assumed, by some writers, that these bodies are
co-partnerships, yet a critical examination of the cases decided will prove that they are not co-partnerships, although,
as will be shown further on, they do have some of the at-
tributes of, and for certain purposes are treated as, co-
partnerships.

It would seem that the fact of their not being corporations and not being joint stock companies, nor yet simply
individuals, and acting as such, has been the occasion for
calling them co-partnerships, the writers who have done so
being evidently at a loss for any other applicable classifica-
tion.

It will be remembered that many of these bodies are formally incorporated, and thereby become subject to the laws
of incorporations, yet very many, probably a large majority, remain unincorporated, and it is more particularly in
regard to the nature of the latter class that this section per-
tains. Examining now the authorities, they are substan-
tially as follows :

In one it is assumed, without argument, that the members of a club, formed for social purposes, are not
partners.[1]

In one of the latest and most important cases,[2] it was
sought to hold personally and individually liable the members of a masonic lodge for debts incurred in building their
temple. The decision was that this could not be done ; the

[1] Waller v. Thomas, 42 How. Pr. 344.
[2] Ash v. Guie, 70 Pa. St. 493; s. c., 39 Am. R. 816.

court was of the opinion that in order to constitute a partnership, "there must be a community of interests for business purposes. Hence, voluntary associations or clubs, for social and charitable purposes, and the like, are not proper partnerships, nor have their members the powers and responsibilities of partners." Whilst thus the members were not liable on the mere ground of membership for those debts, yet all those who engaged in the enterprise, all who assented thereto, all who ratified it, in fact all who voted for or advised the construction of the building, together with the committee in charge of the matter, were held personally liable for the debts. Especially were those to be held personally liable who issued what purported to be a certificate of indebtedness, those who advised this step, and those who advised the affixing of the lodge seal to the certificate.

A very recent case in the highest court of New York,[1] states clearly the underlying distinctions thus: "Associations of this description are not usually partnerships. There is no power to compel payment of dues, and the right of the member ceases when he fails to meet his annual subscription. This certainly is not a partnership, and the rights of co-partners as such are not fully recognized. The purpose is not business, trade or profit, but the benefit and protection of its members, as provided for in its constitution and by-laws. In accordance with well established rules, no partnership exists under such circumstances." It was accordingly decided that the court would not dissolve a lodge of the Order of Rechabites, although it had accumulated more property than it needed, and parts of its hall, by being sub-let, were the source of considerable revenue, the purpose was held to be, nevertheless, benevolent; nor would the court interfere on account of the hostility of the members towards each other, albeit their object was "mutual benefit in the exercise of temperance, fortitude and justice," together with relief and assistance in times of sickness and death.

[1] Lafond v. Deems, 81 N. Y 514.

Yet in the same State, but in one of the lower courts,[1] a number of gentlemen forming a club were treated as a partnership to the fullest extent, and held liable for the debts of the club. The rule applicable was declared to be that of partnerships, and each member liable until he gives public notice of withdrawal.

The English rule is to the effect that a mutual beneficial society partakes more of the character of a club than of a trading association.[2] Distinguishing thus, that in a trading association, or partnership, one member can incur debts which will be binding on his partners, although the debts be incurred in direct violation of an agreement with them, provided, of course, that the debts were incurred within the real or apparent scope of the partnership business; but in beneficial associations, clubs, etc., the acting committees which incur debts are considered to be merely the agents of the collective body of members behind them, and any one dealing with such committees must first ascertain the extent of their powers, from an inspection of the constitution, rules and proceedings of such association.

The plaintiff and the defendant[3] were both members of a society, formed for the purpose of protecting trade by issuing reports of failures, etc.; the defendant, as a committee man, engaged plaintiff to do the printing for the society, and the latter was allowed to maintain his suit against the former personally for the printing bill.

MARTIN, B.: "Here is a number of persons associated together, and subscribing each a small sum annually for the purpose of obtaining information which may be useful in their business; it is an abuse of terms to call this a partnership." (The other question in the case was, as in most . other cases, whether plaintiff, when he undertook the work, gave credit to the defendant or to the society; of course if to the latter he could not have held the former, but it was

---

[1] Park v. Spaulding (Worth Club Case), 10 Hun. 131.

[2] Fleming v. Hector, 2 M. & W. 172.

[3] Caldicott v. Griffiths, 22 Eng. L. & Eq. 527.

decided on the facts that he did the work on defendant's credit.)[1]

Another ground of distinction can be seen to be this : If a partner dies, the partnership is dissolved ; but if a member of one of these associations dies, it has no effect on the association ; they are, therefore, not to be judged either as corporations, joint stock associations or co-partnerships.[2]

In *Thomas* v. *Ellmaker*,[3] the topic is very fully discussed by the counsel and the court, and it is decided that a Hose Company is not a partnership, that the court would not dissolve it and divide the assets, especially not on application of the minority. The property was said to be pledged for the object for which it had been given, and was not to be diverted whilst there were those ready to execute the public trust with which it had been clothed.

§ 3. **For some purposes treated as Co-Partnerships.**— Although these bodies are not co-partnerships, nevertheless they are for some purposes treated as such, thus COLLYER, in his work on partnerships, says : Section 53. "There are some societies not engaged in trade, but which not partaking of a corporate character, are dealt with in a court of equity as partnerships, as private societies for the relief of members in cases of sickness, etc."

And there are several cases in which the courts simply assume that they are partnerships, and deal with them as such.

Thus[4] the American Mutual Exemption Society, which had been formed to raise funds to free its members from the military draft, had later been dissolved, and it was decided that each member could sue the treasurer for his individual, and ascertained, share of the fund ; it was said

---

[1] See also Ebbinghausen v. Worth Club, 4 Abb. (N. C.) 300.

[2] This topic is quite fully considered in White v. Brownell, found in 3 Abb. Pr. R. (N. S.) 325; 4 Id. 189: 2 Daly, 355. See also Olery v. Brown, 51 How. Pr. 92.

[3] 1 Parsons Select Cases, 98.

[4] Koehler v. Brown, 2 Daly (N. Y.) 78.

that the association had not been formed under any general or special law of the legislature, and was, therefore, simply a partnership.

A mutual marine insurance society is treated as a partnership,[1] for the purpose of determining whether a member had been rightfully expelled or not.

Where the articles of association had been disregarded,[2] the court considered a mutual society for insurance of property as a general partnership, for the purpose of adjusting the rights of members against each other.

The Riggers and Stevedors Union Association, of San Francisco, was organized for the purpose of giving pecuniary assistance to disabled or sick members, and also to defray funeral expenses. · Plaintiffs were expelled for refusing to take an oath, the imposition of which had not been authorized by the constitution or by-laws. The court refused to dissolve the association, but ordered that the expelled members be reinstated.[3] The opinion states that the association is a partnership, and a court would dissolve it upon the same grounds of bad faith and mismanagement as would suffice to dissolve a partnership, but that the court would not dissolve the association if the objectionable oath would be withdrawn. Upon the point of partnership it was said : " We do not see why a number of persons capable of contracting may not associate and agree, as the basis and consideration of the association, that the funds raised by voluntary contributions or otherwise, through the by-laws of the company, shall be appropriated absolutely or in a given contingency to the benefit of the individual members." * * * * "This is not a charity any more than an assurance society against fire or upon life is a charity. It is simply a fair and reciprocal contract among the

---

[1] Wood v. Woad, L. R. 9 Exch. 190; 10 Eng. R. (Moak), 372.

[2] Ellison v. Bignold, 2 Jacob & Walker, 503. In Brown v. Dale, Law R. 9 Ch. Div. 78, 25 Eng. R. (Moak), 776, the "Fellowship of Fullers and Dyers" is treated as a partnership for the purpose of making the division of a fund among the members.

[3] Gorman v. Russell, 14 Cal. 532, 18-688.

members to pay certain amounts in certain contingencies to
each other, but out of a common fund."

Among the English cases which are cited in the last
named, there is one[1] in which a Benevolent Union Society,
organized for the relief of the members in case of sickness,
was considered as a mere partnership for the purpose of
making some of the members account for the proceeds of
property (stocks) of the association sold by them without
authority.

And in another[2] it was declared that a sick relief society
is a mere partnership, and if it appears to be a mere bubble,
the courts will dissolve it, and they will dissolve any
friendly society formed on erroneous principles, and tem-
porarily restrain payments which would exhaust the funds.

In *Babb* v. *Reed*,[3] there were members of an Odd Fellows Society who had claims for work, etc., upon the hall;
there were other parties, not members, who also had claims,
and it was decided that those who were not members, were
entitled to priority in payment out of a fund arising from a
sale of the building. It was also stated that all who were
members at the time the debts to the non-members were incurred, would be jointly and severally liable for their payment, but as this question was not really before the court,
and its decision not directly involved in the case, the utter-
ance thereon must be regarded merely as *obiter dictum*, and
hence not really binding as a precedent.

A board of brokers is not strictly a corporation, partnership or joint stock company, but a voluntary association,
and, in respect to their powers of expulsion, etc., subject
to the control of the courts, exercised in the same general
manner as towards corporations, and will be enjoined from
improperly expelling a member.[4]

§ 4. **Are they Public Charities?**— The question has been
raised occasionally whether the various fraternities are char-

---

[1] Beaumont v. Meredith, 3 Vesey & Beames, 180.
[2] Pierce v. Piper, 17 Vesey, 15.
[3] 5 Rawle, 159.
[4] Leech v. Harris, 2 Brewst. (Pa.) 571.

itable institutions to the extent of having their property free from taxation, the same as hospitals, churches, etc. It is quite unnecessary to say that the point is a very important one. When it will be considered that there are in the country from thirty to fifty of the Supreme Directories, or lodges, which in turn have Grand or State organizations, and these again innumerable subordinate lodges, all of which hold more or less real or personal property, it will be evident that taxation if imposed would amount to a great deal.

There are conflicting decisions in relation to this subject.

The question came fairly before the court in Indiana, and it was decided[1] that the property of a masonic body was not subject to taxation, because the statute exempted every building erected for the use of any benevolent or charitable institution, and it was said:

"If that only be charity which relieves human want, without discrimination amongst those who need relief, then indeed it is a rarer virtue than has been supposed. And if one organization may confine itself to a sex, a church, or city, why not to a given co-fraternity?"

But in another State directly the contrary conclusion was arrived at in relation to the property of Odd Fellows, the court deciding the case without giving any argument or reasoning upon it.[2]

The question was also considered, and very thoroughly, in *Bangor v. Masonic Lodge*,[3] and it was held that the lodge was not within the meaning of the statute which exempted charitable institutions from taxation. The lodge was said to be a society for mutual benefit and protection, and the ends to be attained private and personal, not public.

But where the lodges had for seventy years been treated as exempt by the taxing officers, the court refused to put a

[1] Indianapolis v. Grand Master, 25 Indiana, 518.
[2] Morning Star Lodge v. Hayslip, 23 Ohio St. 144.
[3] 73 Maine, 429; 40 Am. R. 369.

different meaning upon the law than that which the taxing power had itself for so long a time attached thereto.[1]

Other cases give decisions showing the nature of these bodies, but the foregoing are thought to be all which involved directly the matter of taxation.

Probably a case[2] which goes the farthest towards establishing these bodies on the same footing as public charities, related to a masonic lodge (unincorporated). According to a by-law, "the furniture and funds of the lodge shall be considered as the joint and equal property of all the members, who shall, by a majority of votes, have the management thereof for the good of the craft, or for the relief of indigent and distressed worthy masons, their widows and orphans." By a vote of the lodge the same was dissolved, and the funds ordered to be distributed among the members. Plaintiff demanded his share from the treasurer. The court found that the funds had accumulative during many years; that they were for a *charitable use*, and could not be divided among the members. It was said, furthermore, that the lodge could, of course, be dissolved, but that in such case the courts would, on proper application, appoint a trustee to take possession of the fund, and administer it for the use for which it had accumulated, that is, "for the good of the craft, or for relief of indigent or distressed worthy masons, their widows and orphans."

In Alabama in a case[3] in which a lodge sued for money, it was objected that a mason could not be on the jury, but the court decided that he could, because the masonic body was a public charity, and being such, one of its own members was not disqualified to act as juror. The court declared that it would take judicial notice of the fact that it was thus a purely public charity. "The society known as Free Masons has long existed in this country, and in almost every part of it. The purpose and object of the society has been

[1] State v. Addison, 2 S. C. 499. See also Mayor v. Solomon's Lodge, 53 Ga. 93.
[2] Duke v. Fuller, 9 N. H. 536.
[3] Burdine v. Grand Lodge, 37 Ala. 478.

made public in numerous books, periodicals and public addresses. From all these sources of information, and from the generally received and accredited judgment of the public, the sole purpose and object with which masonic institutions acquire money and property, beyond their current expenses as a society (furniture, light, fuel, stationery, and the like), are for the bestowal of reliefs and charities to the needy. In addition, the third and fourth sections of the act to incorporate masonic lodges in the State of Alabama, tend to confirm the belief that the society is eleemosynary in its aim."

A society had been formed in the usual manner for the accumulation of funds by contributions from the members, and for their relief when sick. The law of the State required that devises for "charitable uses" be made at least one month before the death of the testator. Mrs. Swift, only a week before her death, made her will, by which she left $1,000 to the society. It was decided that the sum was not left to a charitable use and that the society should have it.[1]

In England, also, it has been decided[2] that a similar legacy was not for a charitable use. It had been given to the "Ringwood Friendly Society," organized for mutual relief in the usual manner. The society having been dissolved, the fund from the legacy still being in the hands of the trustees, was claimed by the descendants of the testator. The attorney-general, on the other hand, claimed that the society had been formed for charitable purposes, and, inasmuch as it had been dissolved, the legacy would have to be turned over to some other charitable organization as nearly like the first in character as possible (according to the doctrine of cy-pres), but the court decided that the funds had not originally been given for a charitable use, and that the testator's descendants were entitled to them.

The Kennebec Masonic Relief Association was held[3] to be a mutual life insurance company, notwithstanding that it

---

[1] Swift v. Easton Beneficial Society, 73 Pa. St. 362.
[2] Clark's Trust, before Hall, V. Ch. 1875: 16 Eng. R. (Moak.) 624.
[3] Bolton v. Bolton, 73 Maine, 299.

is benevolent, and not speculative, in its purpose. If the prevalent purpose and nature of an association, of whatever name, be that of insurance, the benevolent or charitable results to its beneficiaries would not change its legal character. In this case the question was to determine to whom the fund was payable.

Gorman v. Russell, stated a few pages back, shows that the Riggers and Stevedors Union was not a charity.

In *Everett v. Carr*,[1] it was decided that a legacy said to be for a charitable purpose, could validly be given to a masonic lodge which was duly incorporated with power, among others, "to take and hold for charitable and benevolent uses," real and personal estate.

Any one interested in ascertaining what are and what are not institutions of purely public charity, may examine with profit the case of *County of Hennepin v. Brotherhood*, etc.,[2] as reported in 38 American Reports, 298, where is appended a very valuable note.[3]

§ 5. **Are they Insurance Companies?**—Whether or not these various orders, associations and societies are insurance companies, and subject to the insurance laws of a State, has been determined in several instances. In reference to this matter the bodies concerned were, as a rule, regularly incorporated.

In the case of the *State v. Bankers' and Merchants' Mutual Benevolent Association*,[4] the defendant was held to be an insurance company, but on the co-operative plan, and, therefore, could not be required to deposit $100,000 with

---

[1] 59 Maine, 326.

[2] 27 Minn. 460.

[3] Citing McDonald v. Mass. Gen. Hospital, 120 Mass. 432; Clement v. Hyde, 50 Vt. 716; Warde v. Manchester, 56 N. H. 508; Burd, etc. v. School Dist., 90 Pa. St. 21; Philadelphia v. Fox, 64 Pa. St. 169; Donohugh's Appeal, 86 Pa. St. 306; Gerke v. Purcell, 25 Ohio St. 229; Humphries v. Little Sisters of the Poor, 29 Ohio St. 201; Vidal v. Girards Ex'rs., 2 How. 128; President v. Drummond, 7 H. L. C. 141; Trustees of British Museum v. White, 2 Sim. & Stu. 595; Jones v. Williams, 2 Amb. 652; Jackson v. Phillips, 14 Allen, 539; American Academy of Fine Arts, etc. v. Harvard College, 12 Gray, 583.

[4] 23 Kansas, 499.

the State Treasurer ; and it was so determined, although the association required from its members deposits as guaranty for assessments, and used the interest arising from said deposits, and used, also, forfeited deposits, in lieu of assessments, as far as possible.

An incorporation " for the purpose of mutual protection and relief of its members, and for the payment of stipulated sums of money to the families or heirs of deceased members," was held not subject to the insurance laws of Ohio.[1]

The National Mutual Aid Association, organized under the laws of Ohio, is not included in the act of Pennsylvania which taxes foreign insurance companies.[2]

An association,[3] being intended only for the benefit of widows, orphans, heirs and devisees of deceased members, no annual dues being required, and the members receiving no money as profit, or otherwise, while it is an insurance company, is such a one as under the statutes of Illinois is exempted from depositing a guarantee fund ; and this is so, although the members are subject to assessment for annual expenses, and although the officers, who are also members, are paid for their services.

Individuals associated together by no other tie than that of mutual indemnity, having paid officers, giving premiums for new members, and in which the sole condition of membership is health and probable duration of life, are engaged in insurance, and must conform to the insurance laws of Missouri.[4] And this is so although the amount of insurance is uncertain, being dependent on mutual assessment, and the policy not assignable, but payable only to the widow, heirs or devisees. In cases, however, in which the primary

[1] State v. The Mutual Protection Association of Ohio, 26 Ohio St. 19.

[2] Commonwealth v. N. M. A. A., 94 Pa. St. (13 Norris), 481.

[3] Commercial League Association v. People, 90 Ill. 166.

[4] State, rel. Beach v. Citizens' Benefit Association, 6 Mo. App. 163; also in full in 6 Central Law Journal, 491. See, also, to the same effect, State v. Merchants Exchange Mutual Benevolent Society, 72 Mo. 146; the opinion and arguments in this case are very instructive.

object of an association is of a benevolent, literary or social nature, to which a feature of mutual insurance is added, then it would be a question still to be decided, whether or not there would have to be compliance with the State insurance laws.

Under the peculiarities of the Iowa Statutes,[1] an association, though having as its sole object the insurance of its members, was held not obliged to conform to the general insurance laws.[2]

An association to relieve the sick and to pay to members over seventy-five years old a certain benefit, does not come under the general insurance laws.[3]

An association which pays half the total amount of the policy at the expiration of two-thirds of the life expectancy of the member, and which, having no capital, depends solely upon a system of voluntary assessments and contributions, need not conform to the deposit laws of New York.[4]

An agent of the Connecticut Mutual Benefit Company was held properly convicted of the offense of soliciting life insurance without first obtaining authority.[5] On the death of a member the company was to pay as many dollars as there were members, but members were not obliged to pay assessments, and if they failed the result was simply to end their policies. The defendant insisted, under these facts, that the object of the company was benevolent, and not speculative, still the court held that the company was an insurance company within the meaning of the statute, and that defendant was guilty of soliciting insurance without State authority.[6]

[1] State v. Iowa, M. A. A., 12 N. W. R. 782.
[2] State v. Iowa, etc., supra.
[3] Supreme Council of Chosen Friends v. Fairman, 10 Ab. N. C. 162; s. c., 62 How. Pr. (N. Y.) 386.
[4] People v. Mutual Endowment and Accidental Association, Sup. Ct. N. Y.; Ins. L. J., Nov. 1882; Am. L. Review, 1883, p. 136.
[5] Commonwealth v. Wetherbee, 105 Mass. 149.
[6] See also, on these points, Bolton v. Bolton, 73 Maine, 299, stated on page 11, supra.

The New York act providing for the incorporation of societies for "benevolent, charitable, literary, etc., purposes," cannot be used by the "Mutual Reliance Society," which claimed to be formed for the benevolent object of providing a relief fund in the nature of insurance by means of contributions, and of assisting people to obtain insurance. The court says:[1] "This is evidently a corporation for business purposes, having in view pecuniary gain and profit to the corporators. It may contemplate the promotion of the temporal interests of others, but such object is merely incidental to the chief object of the association."

Neither can a savings bank be organized under such statutes. It is said that a savings bank is not charitable, though it promotes economy and providence in the depositors; "any useful employment directly or indirectly benefits others than the persons employed, but if it be carried on for the pecuniary profit of such persons, it is never spoken of as benevolent or charitable."[2]

Upon this point it may be of interest to determine whether these bodies can be deemed as organized for pecuniary profit, especially as this, or a similar phrase, is often met with in the various statutes of the States. A very good definition and explanation of the same is given in *Bear v. Bromley.*[3] The statute required the registration of any joint stock society of more than twenty-five members established for purpose of profit. A "Mutual Friends Society" was held not to be subject to the provisions of this statute, although it had a joint stock fund, raised by subscription, which it loaned to its members, namely, to the highest bidders. The reason and the rule of distinction is given by Lord CAMPBELL, C. J. "The rule," * * * * "is to ascertain whether the profit is a profit to be obtained by the society as such, not whether any individual member is a gainer or loser by its transactions. This is not such a

[1] People v. Nelson, 46 N. Y. 477; also in 3 Lans. N. Y. 324; 10 Ab. Pr. (N. S.) 200.
[2] Sheren v. Mendenhall, 23 Minn. 92.
[3] 11 Eng. Law and Eq., 414.

society. When all the transactions of the society are wound
up, some of the members may gain and some may lose, but
the society would gain nothing."

And by ERLE, J. :   "As between themselves the members of this society have made a profitable investment of
their money, but externally they gain nothing. The deal-
ings of the society are exclusively with the members for
the benefit of the members."

Ellison v. Bignold,[1] presents another test, thus :   A voluntary association for insurance of property by way of mutual guarantee is or is not illegal according as the shares of
the money laid up are or are not transferable generally to
persons not members.

LIABILITY OF MEMBERS.

§ 6. **Personal Liability of Members.**— The members of
these associations are not liable as partners ; these irregularly constituted bodies are treated as partnerships for some
purposes only, and not for all. Still the members are often
individually and personally liable for the debts, and the following is thought to be the rule which determines the point,
namely : If the society, either by rule or custom, allows its
officials or servants to incur debts, then all members would
become personally liable, and, of course, where the entire
organization is on a credit principle, every member would be
liable ; but if the society works on a cash basis, then the
mere fact of membership would not make one personally
liable for the debts ; yet, as shown in *Ash v. Guie, supra*, a
member would be personally liable for any debt, the incur-
ring of which he has advised, sanctioned or ratified.

As illustrating the foregoing, the case of *Cockerell v.
Aucompte*,[2] holds the members of a " coal club " individually liable for coal furnished to the club, because an examination of the rules and entire system of the club convinced
the court that it was intended to allow the officials to buy on

---

[1] 2 Jacob & Walker, 503.
[2] 40 Eng. Law and Eq., 284.

credit. The cases of *Fleming v. Hector* and *Todd v. Emly* are distinguished; in these the members were not liable, it appearing that the stewards were confined to a cash basis. In such cases, as was stated by Lord St. Leonards:[1] "It is very clearly settled that no member of a club is liable to creditors of a club, except so far as by contract or dealing he may have made himself personally liable; and this is mere common sense, for, if a member paying his annual subscription and paying for the articles which he orders in the club, was also liable to pay the person who supplied the club with those articles, who would belong to a club?"

The officers of a masonic lodge borrowed money on a note and used the same for lodge purposes. It was held that all the members who approved or ratified the making of the note, were personally liable for the same.[2]

A member of the "New England Pigeon and Bantam Society,"[3] is not personally liable for premiums offered by the committee, it not appearing that he was present when the committee was appointed, or that the same was ever authorized to offer premiums.

The members of the "Thespian Society," a theatrical club, were held not liable on a rent contract made by some of their predecessors in the club, and that if they could be held at all, it would be only for use and occupation.[4]

---

[1] In The St. James Club, 16 Jur. 1075. But the members of the Worth Club were held personally liable; see Park v. Spaulding, 10 Hun (N. Y.) 131.

[2] Ferris v. Thaw, 72 Mo. 446. But to be personally held, trustees must in some way incur individual liability. Wolf v. Schlieffer, 2 Brewst. Pa. 563. Odd Fellows were held not personally liable for $30 for funeral, at the suit of the claimant; if liable at all, they would be so at the suit of the lodge; see Payne v. Snow, 12 Cush. (Mass.) 443. Suspended Odd Fellows are liable to the lodge for dues which, by signing the constitution, they agree to pay, and can be sued at law for the same; see Palmetto Lodge v. Hubbell, 2 Strobh. (S. C.) 457. Payment of assessments were held not obligatory upon members of the insolvent Protection Life Ins. Co.; see 9 Biss. (C. Ct.) 188.

[3] Volger v. Ray, 131 Mass. 439.

[4] Barry v. Nuckolls, 5 Humph. Tenn. 326.

In *Sizer v. Daniels*,[1] it was held that the members of a committee of a political party who voted for a resolution whereby a campaign worker was employed became personally liable for his pay; as did also all other members who ratified the act; and the expiration of the terms of office did not excuse such members, nor make their successors liable for such debt. So also are the members of the political "Morgan and Webb Association," who advised or approved of giving a ball, personally liable for the supper furnished at the same.[2]

The members of a Lyceum are personally liable for a debt incurred for books ordered by a committee appointed to subscribe for them,[3] the court not caring to consider whether they formed a co-partnership or not. All members of a club with whose concurrence plate is purchased, are liable for cost of the same.[4] A subscriber to a fund for an academy building is personally liable to a builder hired by him, although he called himself agent for the subscribers when dealing with the builder.[5] But where plaintiff also was a subscriber, it was decided that he knew that defendant was acting only on behalf of the association, and the defendant was, therefore, not liable to pay plaintiff for his services in hauling lumber to the meeting house, to the building of which they had both subscribed.[6]

Where it was sought to hold some of the subscribers to a meeting house fund liable for work done by another, the court denied the right, saying:[7] "It does not appear that defendants have funds in their hands. In the absence of any express contract or undertaking he, plaintiff, can have no legal or equitable right to look to the personal security

---

[1] 66 Barb. (N. Y.) 429. In Jenne v. Sutton, 14 Vroom. 257, 39 Am. R. 578, the president of a political club, having ordered fire works, was held personally liable to pay a person injured thereby.

[2] Downing v. Mann, 3 E. D. Smith (N. Y.) 36.

[3] Ridgely v. Dobson, 3 Watts & S. 118.

[4] Delanney v. Strickland, 2 Stark, N. P. 366.

[5] Robinson v. Robinson, 10 Maine, 240.

[6] Abbott v. Cobb, 17 Vt. 597.

[7] Cheeney v. Clark, 3 Vt. 434.

or liability of the defendants, and hold them answerable out of their private funds for work done by him for the benefit of subscribers generally." The case seems to fall under the rule that one of several persons jointly concerned in a common purpose, cannot maintain an action against all or any of the others for work or labor performed for their joint benefit.

Members of a fire engine company voting that one of their number should see to fitting up their rooms, are all, together with him, liable for the debt incurred.[1]

A public meeting appointed a committee to arrange for celebrating the opening of the Erie Canal.[2] This committee, through its agent, engaged the plaintiff, and it was decided that the members of the committee were personally liable to the plaintiff for his pay, on the theory that, " the committee, and not the individuals composing the meeting, are the responsible persons in such cases."

A State Firemens' Association being in need of a well for use at a tournament, the committee on arrangements appointed a sub-committee, which last engaged plaintiff to construct the well. It was decided that the members of the committee were personally liable for the debt.[3] The sub-committee, it was said, could bind the committee, and the members of the latter were liable on the theory that any agent is liable where there is no principal back of him. " Such a rule is salutary and tends to the promotion of justice by preventing the procurement of services from too incautious and confiding laborers, by putting forth an irresponsible committee to act for an irresponsible public gathering."

Of course, where a State Statute has been adopted, it may fix the liabilities of parties on the foregoing, or on a different, basis.

Thus, in New York, the trustees of corporations formed for social and recreative purposes, are by statute per-

---

[1] Newell v. Borden, 128 Mass. 31.

[2] McCartee v. Chambers, 6 Wend. 649.

[3] Fredendall v. Taylor, 23 Wis. 538; s. c., 26 Id. 286. See, also, Secor v. Lord, 4 Abb. N. Y. App. 188.

sonally liable for its debts incurred during their term of
office.[1]

THE POLICY.

It is unnecessary to say that it is of the utmost importance to members to see that their policy, or beneficiary certificate, or whatever else it be called, is sufficient to hold the
association liable ; and, secondly, that it is so disposed of
that the fund resulting therefrom will go to the parties to
whom it is desired that it be paid.

Various cases construing the laws and policies of different associations will soon be given, but first the attention of
the reader (especially of the layman), is called to another
very important point, namely :

§ 7. **Insurable Interest.**— As it has been decided that
the absence of an " insurable interest " avoids a policy in a
beneficiary association, the same as it would a policy in any
regular insurance company,[2] it will now be in order to consider what is meant by this phrase, " insurable interest,"
and any reader of this chapter would do well to see how his
policy stands by its own terms, or on the records of the
association, for, if there is no "insurable interest," there
would be imminent danger that the policy would not, or at
least need not, ever be paid.

The wife has an insurable interest in the life of her husband.[3]   It is not to be presumed that, for the sake of the

---

[1] Hall v. Siegel, 7 Lansing, 206.

[2] Mutual Benefit Association v. Hoyt, Michigan, 1881, 9 N. W. R. 497,
in which the court felt itself most strongly called upon from the circumstances of the case to enforce the policy, but, owing to want of insurable
interest, could not do so.

[3] Which continues after divorce. Conn. M. L. I. Co. v. Schaefer, 94
U. S. 457; Phœnix v. Dunham. 46 Conn. 79; s. c., 33 Am. R. 14. For a
full discussion reference must be to some book on Insurance, but
following cases contain a great deal of information.   It is said that the
mere relation of uncle and nephew, does not constitute an insurable interest.   Singleton v. St. Louis M. I. Co., 66 Mo. 63; s. c., 27 Am. R. 327,
with valuable note.   Neither does the mere relation of parent and child.
Guardian M. L. I. Co. v. Hogan, 80 Ill. 35; s. c., 22 Am. R. 180, but
other cases hold that it does.   Reserve M. I. Co. v. Kane, 81 Pa. St. 154·

money, she will desire his death. Thus also parties standing in other relationships of mutual dependence, may take a valid policy one on the other. A creditor even may hold a policy on the life of his debtor. But it is very evident that if A. B. is nowise related to C. D., and is not his creditor, nor in any manner interested in the continuance of his life, and, nevertheless, takes a policy upon him, then it follows that A. B. would be only benefitted by the death of the other; he would naturally come to await it, and eventually grow quite willing, and perhaps anxious, to have the obsequies occur. There would be no counter desire based on affection or interest to cause him to wish a prolongation of the life of the latter, and every selfish motive would induce him to desire his early death.

The State does not want one person to desire or procure the death of another, and hence, for the protection of the people, and as a matter of public policy, the courts have often declared that they would allow no one to collect insurance on the death of one in whose life he had no "insurable interest." They have also declared that such a policy is a wager, a mere bet, in which the beneficiary is not to be protected or indemnified for any loss he sustains by the death, but in which he merely places a certain sum — bets it — against the higher sum placed by the insurance company, the latter amount to change hands on the happening of the death.

Such insurance is therefore void, because, as stated, it is against public policy by offering a temptation to the taking

s. c., 22 Am. R. 741; Grattan v. L. I. Co., 15 Hun. 74; Mitchell v. Union, 45 Me. 104; Loomis v. Eagle, 6 Gray, Mass. 396. The sister has insurable interest in the brother, Ætna v. France, 94 U. S. 561, if dependent on him, Lord v. Dall, 12 Mass. 115. And a woman in the life of one to whom she is betrothed. Chisholm v. National C. L. I. Co., 52 Mo. 213; s. c., 14 Am. R. 414. The creditor on the debtor. Morrell v. Trenton, 10 Cush. Mass. 282. Succession of Hearing. 26 La. An. 326. Yet policy should not be disproportionately large. Cammack v. Lewis, 15 Wall. 643. The company, however, having paid to the creditor, he must turn it over to the representative of the deceased. Cammack v. Lewis. A person may hold a policy on his business partner. Conn. etc. Co. v. Luchs, U. S. S. C. (1883), 2 S. C. R. 949.

of life ; and it is also void (in most States, perhaps all), because it is a wager or bet. Statutes against wagers are now found in probably all the States.

The various rules and modifications relating to " insurable interest," are not to be expected to be given here in full ; for extensive research some book on Insurance must be examined. It may be stated here that some courts have held that, although A. B. cannot take a policy on C. D., if he have no insurable interest in him, yet that C. D. can, in such case, take a valid policy on his own life and *assign* it to A. B., in whose hands it will remain valid. This view is, however, fully refuted after a careful examination in a recent case of the highest authority, in which the definition of insurable interest is so aptly given that it is here reproduced somewhat at length ; not, of course, so much for the benefit of lawyers who are all familiar with it, but for those who have not access to the law books. The following is the language referred to :

" It is not easy to define with precision what will in all cases constitute an insurable interest so as to take the contract [1] out of the class of wager policies. It may be stated generally, however, to be such an interest arising from the relations of the party obtaining the insurance, either as creditor of or surety for the assured, or from the ties of blood or marriage to him, as will justify a reasonable expectation of advantage or benefit from the continuance of his life. It is not necessary that the expectation of advantage or benefit should be always capable of pecuniary estimation, for a parent has an insurable interest in the life of his child." * * * * " The natural affection in cases of this kind, is considered as more powerful — as operating more efficaciously — to protect the life of the insured, than any other consideration."

§ 8. **Different from ordinary Insurance.**— The policy or beneficiary certificate in the mutual, or benevolent, asso-

---

[1] Warnock v. Davis, Supreme Court of the United States, 104 U. S. 775. See, also, Missouri, etc. v. Sturges, 18 Kansas, 93; *s. c.*, 26 Am. R. 761; but *contra*, Cunningham v. Smith, 70 Pa. St. 450.

ciations, as they are usually called, is considerably different in its nature from the ordinary life insurance policy ; the latter is supposed to be a mere debt payable by the company to the estate of the insured, and collectible at all events from the company by the legal representatives of the insured, or by the parties named in the policy.

This subject was considered in the case of *Ballou v. Gile,*[1] in which it appeared that the "Royal Arcanum" had among its articles the following :

"The object of the order is to establish a widows and orphans benefit fund," * * * "a sum not exceeding $3,000 shall be paid to his (the member's) family or those dependent upon him, as he may direct."

"In case no direction is made by a brother, either by will, entry or benefit certificate, the Council may cause the same to be paid to the person or persons entitled thereto. In case no person or persons are entitled to the benefit, it shall revert back to the widow and orphans benefit fund."

Under these provisions the court decided that, as the deceased had failed to make the designation, the fund belonged to his widow, she being a member of his family and dependent upon him, and that if she were not there to take, the fund would not go to the deceased's administrator for the benefit of creditors (as would an ordinary life insurance policy[2]), but that, in such event, the fund would remain to the association.

The same distinction is clearly shown in the case of *Wor ley v. Northwestern Masonic Aid Association.*[3] The pur-

[1] Wisconsin, 1880, 7 N. W. R. 273. In Fenn v. Lewis, 10 Mo. App. 478, the rule was, that in the absence of direction by the deceased, the money should "be paid to the person or persons entitled thereto," and it was decided that the fund went to the family, and not to the administrator of the deceased. The term "legal representatives" includes those parties mentioned specifically, as, for instance, "widow, orphans, heir or legatees." Masonic etc. v. McAuley, Sup. Ct. Dist. Columbia, Wash. Rep., Nov. 15, 1882; Am. L. Reg., 1883, p. 141.

[2] In many States ordinary life insurance comes to the widow or children free of debts of the deceased, but that is so by force of especial statutes.

[3] U. S. C. C. Iowa, 1882, 10 F. R. 227; s. c., 3 McCrary, 53.

pose of the association was to secure pecuniary aid to the
" widows and orphans, heirs and devisees of deceased members." Deceased had taken a certificate in which it was
stated that the amount should be paid to his " devisees."
There being no will found after his death, there were, of
course, no " devisees." Suit was brought by the administrator, but it was decided that he could not recover. It was
stated that the certificate was not like an ordinary insurance
policy or a promissory note, which would be assets in the
estate of the deceased, and which could be collected by the
administrator (although drawn to the name of deceased, and
not indorsed by him). To suppose these beneficiary policies to be thus general assets, and collectible by an administrator, was said to be " utterly repugnant to the whole purpose, scope and design of the association, as provided in
the very law of its existence."

Therefore, it was held that the administrator could not
recover the money either in his character as representing
creditors, nor could he collect it as representative of the
widow, orphans or heirs. True, the policy *might* have been
made payable to any of these, *or* to the " devisees," but as
it was made payable to the " devisees " without mentioning
any of the others in any manner, they were deemed excluded, and, as there were no " devisees," the fund remained to the association.

In *McClure v. Johnson*,[1] the object of a Free Masons
Protective Association is stated to be " to secure to the
families of deceased members," * * * * " such pecuniary
aid as may be provided." The amount was payable to the
"wife, husband, children, mother, sister, father or brother
of such deceased member, and in the order above named."
The deceased left a will in which he directed that the fund
should be paid to a certain creditor, but the court decided
that it should be paid to the wife ; and this was upon the
ground that the fund was, by the terms of the policy, distinctly payable to her, and that the husband had no power

[1] 56 Iowa, 620.

at all to change the beneficiary, inasmuch as the fund was not payable to him or his representatives in any way.[1]

The case of *Kentucky Masonic M. L. I. Co. v. Miller*,[2] is very significant. The company was authorized by its charter to insure a member for the benefit of his widow and children. The policy, as issued, was made payable to the " heirs " of deceased, who left a widow but no children. The administrator claimed the fund in behalf of the creditors of the deceased, and on the ground that the word " heirs " meant the same as " legal representatives," which would include the administrator. The court decided that the fund belonged to the widow, that the corporation had no authority under its charter to make a policy payable to any one else than the widow and children ; strengthening these conclusions by reference to other clauses of the charter which stated that no part of the stock or interest of any

---

[1] The same rule will be found in many cases on ordinary insurance policies. Thus, if A. B. has a policy on his own life, but payable to C. D., then A. B. *cannot*, in any manner, change the name of the beneficiary; but there are also many authorities which take a contrary view. The following may be consulted with profit on this point: Robinson v. Duvall, 79 Ky. 83; Ricker v. Charter Oak, 27 Minn. 193, also in 38 Am. R. 289, where there is appended a valuable note, citing Brockhaus v. Kemna, 7 F. R. 609; Clark v. Durand, 12 Wis. 83; Kerman v. Howard, 23 Id. 108; Charter Oak v. Brant, 47 Mo. 419; Gambs v. Covenant, 50 Id. 44; Landram v. Knowles, 22 N. J. Eq. 594; Bliss L. Ins., § 317, also 2 Ed., p. 517; Insurance Co. v. Palmer, 42 Conn. 60; Lemon v. Phœnix, 38 Conn. 300; Glanz v. Gloeckler, Ill. App. Ct. 1882; North Am. L. I. Co. v. Wilson, 111 Mass. 542; Ellison v. Ellison, 1 Lead. Cases in Eq., 4th Am. Ed. 421; Fortescue v. Barnett, 2 Myl. & K. 36; Otis v. Beckwith, 49 Ill. 121; Badgely v. Votrain, 68 Ill. 25; Gault v. Trumbo, 17 B. Mon. 682. See, also, Glanz v. Gloeckler, Illinois, 1883, 16 Central Law Journal, 268. A review of these cases, and a very able criticism of those which hold that the beneficiary can not be changed, is given by Emlin McClain, Professor at the Iowa State University, in the Western Jurist, July, 1883, p. 297.

It has been decided that the direction for payment, contained in the certificate of the Knights of Honor, could be changed. Tennessee Lodge v. Ladd, 5 Lea. (Tenn.) 716. Examine also, Durain v. Central etc., 7 Daly (N. Y.) 168, being a case in which, by a change in the constitution of the "Hermans Sons," the fund which was at first payable to the widow, became payable to the person whom the member might designate.

[2] 13 Bush. 489.

member, or of his widow and children, shall be subject to any debt against him or them.

Probably the most instructive case, and one showing the extreme care which is required on the part of members in making disposition of the beneficiary fund, is that of *Maryland M. B. etc. v. Clendinen*.[1] Appellants were the "Improved Order of Red Men," and incorporated "with a view to aid the families of deceased members, and to secure to the widow, child or children of deceased members the sum of one dollar from each member of the association." The deceased left a will in which, after certain dispositions, he *bequeathed the residue of his estate* to A. B. and C. D.

The rule was that the beneficiary fund should be payable "to the widow, child, children, or such person or persons to whom the deceased may have disposed of the same by *will* or assignment."

"If there be no widow, child or children, or the deceased shall have made no disposition by will or assignment," * * * * then the "money shall go to the permanent fund of the association."

Under these provisions it was decided that the money did *not* go to A. B. and C. D., because it was not part of the general estate of the deceased, therefore not embraced in the *residuary clause* in the will. The testator should have *referred* in the will to the power, or to the subject of it (*i. e.*, he should have named the Order of which he was a member, and distinctly stated that his beneficiary amount therein should go to A. B. and C. D). Or else it should have been made to appear that the will would have been inoperative without these funds; instead of this it appeared that the testator had other property, and it was assumed, therefore, that the will referred only to the other property. The fund was, therefore, held to remain to the society itself.

The brief statement of the effect of the last case is simply that certificates in these associations are *not* part of the

[1] 44 Md. 429; also in 22 Am. R. 52.

general estate of the member, but a mere power, or privilege, of the member to direct payment to be made, which power he must specifically execute, and hence, such beneficiary rights are not embraced in general words used in his will. Although this rule seems very strict, and one member of the court dissents, yet it is unanimously followed in the next case in which it is given in relation to an Odd Fellows policy, which was payable to the "widow, children, mother, sister, father or brother, and in the order named, if not otherwise directed by him (the member) previous to his death."

The will of the member devised to his children his "estate and property, real, personal and mixed," but this was held not to embrace the beneficiary amount, which, therefore, was decided to be payable to the widow, and not to the children.[1]

But a conclusion directly opposite to that of the foregoing cases was reached by the Supreme Court of Tennessee; the opinion being written by the eminent Chancellor Cooper. These conflicting decisions were delivered about the same time, and it is likely that the courts were ignorant of each others decisions. In this case[2] a certificate for $2,000 in an incorporated benevolent Order was payable "to such person or persons as he (the member) may by will, or entry on the record book of this lodge, or on the face of this certificate, direct." The member made his will disposing of "the balance of all my property of every kind." It was said that these words "are as broad as could possibly be used to pass the residuum of an estate. The only question, therefore, is, was this fund part of the testator's estate at his death, when the will speaks as to personalty? And of this there cannot be a particle of doubt."

On this matter of "property," and to determine what that word means, and whether it embraces these beneficiary certificates, it would be well to read a recent English

[1] Arthur v. Odd Fellows, B. A. 29 Ohio St. 557.
[2] Weil v. Trafford, 3 Tenn. Ch. 108.

case,[1] which explains the word "property" very thoroughly
(and holds that a pension is included therein, and passes to
the assignee in bankruptcy).

In *Supreme Council v. Priest*,[2] the fund was payable to
the person named by the member, and "entered by his
order in the Society's Will Book." A member made the
proper order on this book, but afterwards, and without any
change in the order on the book, he made a will giving the
fund to a different person. The court held that the person
named in the will was entitled to the fund, and the one
named in the "Will Book" of the society was not entitled,
saying: "Very clear and binding provisions must be shown
to deprive a person of the right given him by the laws of
the land to dispose of such a fund by his last will."

The court found further that under the provisions of the
act of incorporation, the fund was not subject to the debts
of the deceased, and not a part of his general estate, therefore it was not to be turned over to the administratrix, and
by her turned over to the person named in the will, but was
to be directly turned over to the latter.

It would seem that this opinion is slightly self contradic-
tory, if the fund was of such a peculiar nature that it was
not subject to the general rules of property and to general
administration, it would seem that the other peculiar provision, namely, the one requiring the entry on the "Society's
Will Book," should also have been adhered to, and that the
same should have been deemed superior to the designation
in the will. It would appear also from the case of *Worley
v. Northwestern M. A. A.*, stated a few pages back, that
the peculiar provisions adopted by these associations, are
superior to the ordinary rules of property.

Another case concerning wills is that of *Greeno v.
Greeno*.[3] Deceased was a member of a Conductors Life
Insurance Company. The by-law provided that "the pre-

---

[1] *Ex parte*, Huggins, Eng. Ct. App. 47 L. T. R. (N. S.) 559; 28
Albany, L. J. 6.

[2] 46 Mich. 429; *s. c.*, 9 N. W. R. 481.

[3] 23 Hun. (N. Y.) 481.

mium to be paid in case of the death of any member of this company, may be disposed of by his last will and testament; otherwise it shall belong to and be paid to his widow." The premium was to be raised in the usual way by an assessment of one dollar upon all surviving members. Deceased named certain legacies in his last will, and then bequeathed " all his personal estate according to the provisions of the statute for the distribution of the personal estates of intestates." But it was decided that this clause in the will did *not* embrace the conductor's insurance, and that the same belonged entirely to the widow.[1]

The difference between lodge and ordinary insurance is further shown in *Richmond v. Johnson*,[2] in which deceased belonged to the A. O. U. W. Members had the right " to hold, dispose of, and fully control said benefit at all times." The certificate was drawn payable to the wife of deceased, but she died before he did. The fund was paid into court by the Order, and was contested for by the administrator of the husband and the administrator of the wife. The court decided that, while in case of ordinary insurance a policy made payable to the wife would have been irrevocable, and would have entitled *her* administrator to the money, even if she had died before the insured (her husband), yet that in this kind of insurance, inasmuch as the member had the right at all times " to hold, dispose of and control the benefit," his mere designation making it payable to her would be revocable. Therefore, her interest in the fund was a mere expectancy, not property, nor estate, it terminated at her death, occurring prior to his, and all her interest was thus extinguished; consequently, the money was directed to be paid to the administrator of the husband.

§ 9. **Enforcement and Forfeiture of the Policy.**— Several decisions show how a policy is to be enforced, and

---

[1] Examine also, Duval v. Goodson, 1880, Kentucky.

[2] Minnesota, 1881, 10 N. W. R. 596. See also, Expressmen's Aid Society v. Fenn, 9 Mo. App. 412; and Masonic etc. v. McAuley, *supra*, in which it was held that the wife was to be considered as the beneficiary only in case she survived her husband.

others, how it is forfeited or lost; these topics occur again in the review of those cases, which relate to the jurisdiction of courts and to the expulsion of members, on subsequent pages.

As it is quite common to provide in these associations for the payment to the representative of the deceased of one dollar, or whatever it be, to be obtained from each member, the question necessarily arises, whether the society is bound absolutely to pay a sum equal to one dollar from each, or whether it need only levy the assessment and pay the result of the same, whether the full amount is made up or not.

In a recent case,[1] the certificate entitled the member "to the benefit of said association in the sum of one dollar for each contributing member," the association, when sued, insisted that it could be required only to make an assessment and to pay the result thereof, whatever it might be, to the plaintiff, but the court decided that the force of the certificate was a contract of absolute payment, and that the association (without regard to the result of its assessment) must pay on the certificate a sum equal to one dollar for each member, the membership being taken at the date of the death of the insured.

So in another instance,[2] in which the certificate called for eighty cents to be paid to the beneficiary for each outstanding certificate, the association defended a suit for the amount, and urged that plaintiff could only ask that the association levy the assessment and pay over the result of the same; this view prevailed in the lower court, but the Supreme Court reversed the ruling, and decided that the certificate was an absolute contract to pay, and that the association must pay the amount, irrespective of the result of an assessment.

But where an assessment was to be made for as many dollars as there were policy holders, and the sum collected

[1] Nerskin v. Northwestern Endowment Legacy Association (Minn. 1883), 15 N. W. R. 683.
[2] Burland v. Northwestern Mutual Benefit Association, 47 Michigan, 424; 11 N. W. R. 269.

was to be paid within ninety days from filing proof of death, it was decided that the plaintiff in a suit must allege that the association had failed to make the assessment.[1]

Yet again it was decided that where the terms of the rule were that an assessment shall be made, the plaintiff need not state that it had been, because the court would so presume.[2]

The general incidents of these policies are pretty much the same as those of other contracts; thus, where the benefit is payable only to members while in "good standing," they will be presumed, without proof, to be in good standing, and it devolves upon the association to show that they were not.[3] This is analogous to the general rule which will not presume fault in any one. It has, however, been decided that the plaintiff must do more than simply state that a certain amount is due him when suing for benefits; he must set forth the rules of the association and aver that he has complied with them.[4]

As members usually make their payments to the subordinate lodges, which in turn remit to the grand lodges, the question has occurred whether a member would lose his insurance in case he paid to his lodge, and that lodge failed to remit. Evidently the answer is found in the following consideration: If the lower lodge is the agent of the member, and fails to remit, then such failure is chargeable against the member, for it is a rule of law that any one is to be charged with the neglect of his agent; but if the lower lodge is to be regarded as the agent of the higher lodge (just as a local insurance agent is the agent of the company which he represents), then, and in such case, the fault of such lower lodge could not be charged against the members. To determine whose agent the lower lodge really is, depends, of course, upon the wording of the constitutions, by-

[1] Curtis v. Mutual Benefit Co., 48 Conn. 98.
[2] Fairchild v. Northeastern M. I. A., 51 Vt. 613.
[3] Supreme Lodge Knights of Honor of the World v. Johnson, 78 Indiana, 110.
[4] Beneficial Society v. White, 30 N. J. L. 313.

laws, rules and customs of these associations, but as they
all work pretty much upon the same general plan, the cases
decided as to some may be read with profit as to all.

In two cases where this question has arisen, it has been
decided that the lower lodge is the agent of the higher·
lodge, and that, therefore, when the member has paid to
the lower lodge he is to be protected, although the money
has not been sent to the higher lodge.[1] Both of these cases
concerned the " United Ancient Order of Druids." The
first shows that the lower lodge is the agent of the higher for
the purpose of collecting the assessments, and second shows
that it is also the agent for the purpose of fixing the terms
of the contract of insurance with the member.

The right to the beneficiary fund is lost by failing to pay
the requisite dues at the times fixed by the rules, charter
and by-laws. And there is this peculiarity about *mutual*
companies, namely, the members are presumed to know,
and are absolutely bound by, the rules of the company, although they may, indeed, be ignorant of their terms, and
although there may be usage and custom in conflict therewith. This is a point of great importance, and should be
carefully examined. Suppose payments are, by the rules,
to be made at a fixed time, and that the company is not required to make any further demand for them, or to give
any further notice that they are due ; suppose, however,
that the company *has* been in the habit of sending out
notices to the members, from time to time, requesting payment, nevertheless, if the company ceases to send notice,
and the member fails to make payment, he will be deemed
in default, and will lose his insurance.[2] The reason why
the custom cannot control the written rule concerning notice
is so plainly stated in a decision by the United States Su-

[1] Schunck v. Gegenseitiger Wittwen and Waisen Fond, 44 Wis. 369.
And Barbaro v. Occidental Grove, *et al.*, 4 Mo. App. 429. See also,
Erdman v. Mutual Ins. Co. ("Hermans Sons"), 44 Wis. 376.

[2] Mutual Fire Ins. Co. v. Miller Lodge, 58 Maryland, 463. Although
this is an instance of mutual fire insurance, there is no reason for not
applying the same doctrines to mutual life insurance.

preme Court,[1] that an extract of the same will be here given, chiefly for the benefit of those who may not have access to the report of the case. The court, in that case, says that the plaintiff "sets up a usage, on the part of the insurance company, of giving notice of the day of payment, and the reliance of the assured upon having such notice. This is no excuse for non-payment. The assured knew, or was bound to know, when his premiums became due." * * * "The reason why the insurance company gives notice to its members of the time of payment of premiums is to aid their memory and to stimulate them to prompt payment. The company is under no obligation to give such notice, and assumes no responsibility by giving it. The duty of the assured to pay at the day is the same whether notice be given or not." And it was also decided that, although the company had been in the habit of allowing thirty days after the maturity of a premium in which to pay it yet, such usage was not binding on the company, and it could at any time refuse to continue this custom, and terminate the same without notice to the policy holders, and thus declare as forfeited all policies in which the premiums had not been paid promptly at maturity.

Where the rules provide that if a member fails to pay within thirty days after publication of notice of assessment his policy is forfeited, it has been decided that the rule is valid, the court saying: "Stringent as are the rules in ordinary life policies, they should be more rigidly applied in mutual associations."[2]

The members of a mutual company are bound to know the charter, rules and by-laws.[3] And this is so, although no reference is made thereto in the policy.[4] Yet, by the word "rules" there is not meant the regulations adopted by the officers in the transaction of business, such as in-

---

[1] Thompson v. Knickerbocker L. I. Co., 104 U. S. 252.

[2] Madeira v. Merchants, etc. Society, C. C. E. D. Mo. 16 F. R. 749.

[3] Coles v. Iowa State, etc., 18 Iowa, 431.   See also, Mitchell v. Lycoming, 51 Pa. St. 402.

[4] Simeral v. Dubuque, etc., 18 Iowa, 322.

structions to agents, etc., but rather the rules under the
charter and by-laws, whereby the liability and rights of the
members are fixed, which are parts of the laws of the institution.[1]

On the other hand, the association cannot assert the existence of a custom against the member; thus, it was held
that payments made to the financier outside the lodge were
valid, though there was a custom that they should be made
in the lodge meeting, and though the officers of the order
had decided that they must be so made.[2]

When the charter provided that members should, in cases
of assessment, be "notified by the secretary or otherwise,
either by a circular or verbal notice," before they could be
deemed in default for non-payment, it was decided that the
company must prove not only that the notice was mailed
to the member, but also that it was *received* by him.[3]

The general rules of waiver of forfeiture are the same in
association insurance as in ordinary insurance. If there are
good reasons for forfeiting a policy, and if the company,
with full knowledge of all the facts, continues to deal with
the policy as though it were valid, it, the company, cannot
thereafter declare it forfeited for such reasons.

Courts, as is well known, do not favor forfeitures, and
will even strain a point to avoid making them.

The Knights of Honor have a rule that a member dying
whilst his lodge is under suspension, is to receive no benefits. At the time of the member's death his lodge was in
default, but it was soon after re-instated, the court[4] decided
that the policy was thereby made payable, and did so by
construing the words, "if a death occur in said lodge during such suspension, no death benefit shall be paid," to
read as though there were annexed to them the words,
"during such suspension."

---

[1] Walsh v. Ætna, 30 Iowa, 145.   See also, Treadway v. Hamilton, 29
Conn. 68.
[2] Manson v. Grand Lodge, A. O. U. W. Minn. 16 N. W. R. 395.
[3] Castner v. Farmers' M. F. I. Co., Michigan. 1883, 15 N. W. R. 452.
[4] Supreme Lodge v. Abbott, 82 Ind. 1.

A member transmitted money as in payment of all his dues, the secretary did not inform him whether it was sufficient or not, therefore it was decided that, although the money was insufficient, yet, the association could not, for the first time after the member's death, make that claim.[1]

When the company knew that the statements in the application were false, and when it still continued to receive the assessments from the insured, it was not allowed thereafter to forfeit the policy.[2] Although a member was still in arrears with some of the preliminary fees, yet the association, having issued him his policy, in which he was declared in good standing, and having twice assessed him thereon, was held obliged to pay the same.[3] The rules of the "Order of Herman's Sons," forfeited a member's insurance, if his assessments were not all paid at the time of his death ; a member died, and thereafter the unpaid assessments were paid to the lodge, and by it remitted to the higher lodge, and this was declared to be a waiver of the forfeiture.[4]

Although as stated, a member must know the rules of the association, and is bound thereby, yet the association may, by special contract with him, waive the same ; thus held in a case in which the membership was restricted to applicants under forty years of age, but as the association received one whom it knew to be over forty, it was bound to pay the insurance upon him.[5]

In other respects there does not seem to be any difference between society and ordinary insurance, it is simply a contract in either case, dependent upon the terms used in drawing it ; thus unless there be a stipulation in the policy, or rules upon the point, it has been held that where a mem-

---

[1] Georgia Masonic M. L. I. Co. v. Gibson, 52 Ga. 640.
[2] Excelsior M. A. A. v. Riddle, Indiana, 1883, 16 Central Law Journal, 407.   See also, Illinois Masonic, etc., v. Baldwin, 86 Ill. 482; Masonic, etc., v. Beck, 77 Indiana, 203, s. c., 40 A. R. 295.
[3] Roswell v. Equitable Aid Union (N. D. N. Y.), 13 F. R. 840.
[4] Erdman v. Mutual Ins. Co., 44 Wis. 376, stated on page 32, *supra*. on the point that lower lodge is agent of the higher.
[5] Olery v. Brown, 51 How. Pr. 92.

ber commits suicide, the association must nevertheless
pay the beneficiary amount,[1] following the rule laid down
for ordinary insurance companies.[2]

The contract is complete when the application is accepted,
which may be by posting a letter, although no certificate has
been issued, the certificate is said to be merely the evidence
of the contract. Where the medical examiner should have
approved the application, but the applicant died before he
did so, the application will be deemed approved, it could not
be arbitrarily rejected, and, other requirements having been
complied with, the contract of insurance was complete.[3]

§ 10. **Miscellaneous Matters Concerning the Policy.**—A
few cases on various topics relating to the Policy are now
given :

In *Folmer's Appeal*,[4] deceased had been a member of the
Penn. Mutual Relief Association. On the death of a member, all survivors were to pay $1, each, to the legal repre-
sentative of the deceased, or to such person as he may have
designated in writing. Provided that where such a member
leaves a widow or children, "he shall have no power to deprive her or them of the benefits specified in this article, by
will or otherwise, but the same shall be paid to her or them
absolutely." The object of the Association was "the relief of widows, orphans or families of deceased members."
When deceased joined the Association, his daughter was
married and lived away from him, but he lived with his sis-
ter-in-law, and in his application made his policy payable to
his niece, and it was decided that the niece and not the
daughter should have the fund. It was said that this was
not a case of depriving the daughter of the fund, because
deceased had never had control of it, but it was from the
first made payable to the niece, the Society had contracted
to that effect, and this was especially the case as deceased

---

[1] Mills v. Robstock, Minn. 1882, 13 N. W. R. 162.

[2] Fitch v. A. P. L. I. Co. 59 N. Y. 573.

[3] Oliver v. Am. Legion of Honor, Sup. Ct. San Francisco, P. C. L. J.
Dec. 9, 1882; Am. L. Rev., 1883, p. 301.

[4] 87 Pa. St. 133.

was a member of the family to which his niece belonged, and he was not of the family to which the daughter belonged.

A fund payable to the widow, is to be paid to the legal widow, and if it has been paid to a concubine, the legal widow may recover it from her.[1] A wife separated from her husband, and not bearing the funeral expenses, was held not entitled to the $25 funeral allowance.[2]

In *Gieger v. McLin*,[3] the rules of a Masonic Mutual life Insurance Company provided as follows: "No part of the stock or interest, which any member, or his widow or children, may have in said institution, shall be subject to any debt, liability or legal or equitable process against him or any of them." By the death of a member, his son became entitled to receive $100, and it was held that said sum was subject to attachment by creditors of the son. The court thought that the interest which was to be exempt from attachment, was that interest which the member possessed in his character as a *stockholder*, and was not the beneficiary amount coming to his representatives, which latter was said to be not an interest "in said institution," but a simple debt from it to the creditors.[4]

That these associations are subject to the same rule governing other insurance companies, which restricts them to the business for which they were organized, and allows them to do no other, is shown very forcibly in *Dietrick v. Madison, Relief Association*.[5] The business of defendant, according to its charter was "to afford relief to the widow

[1] Bolton v. Bolton, 73 Maine. 299; 26 Albany L. J. 280.

[2] Berlin Beneficial Society v. March, 82 Pa. St. 166. But a fund is payable to the person designated, though she be falsely called the wife: Durian v. Central Verein, 7 Daly (N. Y.), 168.

[3] 78 Kentucky, 233.

[4] This seems like a forced conclusion. The words are, "stock or interest," and the parties entitled are "widows or children," which would seem to cover the whole field. Indeed the same court in a prior case considered the words, "stock or interest," as though they were applicable to the beneficiary fund. See Kentucky, etc. v. Miller, 13 Bush. 489, stated on page 25, *supra*.

[5] 45 Wis. 79.

and children of its deceased members and to such business
it shall be limited and restricted." In his application deceased stated that the fund should be paid to his wife. Afterward he borrowed money of the association and assigned
the policy as security to the Association. But it was decided that the Association had no legal power to make a
loan to him, or to accept an assignment from him, that the
same was void, and that the fund belonged to the widow.[1]
Where under the rules an assignment of a policy, in
order to be valid, had to be agreed to by the company, it
was held that an assignment without the requisite consent
of the association thereon indorsed was invalid.[2]   The court
declared this to be a very proper requirement : " The personal character of each holder of a certificate and the interest he holds in the life of the person thereby insured are
essential elements in the contract of mutual indemnity."

JURISDICTION.

Most of the associations, societies and fraternities have
within their organization provision for adjudicating upon
questions arising between the member and the society, and

[1] This was certainly laying down a very strict rule, and it is no wonder
that Ryan, C. J. dissents therefrom.   In Grand Lodge v. Woddill, 36
Ala. 313, it was held that the Grand Lodge of Masons had no power under its charter to loan money, and having loaned, could not recover it.
The tendency of the current decisions is, in cases like this, to allow a
recovery, on the ground that as long as the Government does not complain
of such an act as unauthorized, the person who had the benefit should not
be heard to deny the liability.   See National Bank v. Mathews, 98 U. S.
621 (loan by National Bank on Real Estate).   First N. B. v. Stewart, U.
S. S. C., 1883, (loan on its own stock).   But in Illinois it has been decided that a prohibited loan to directors can not be recovered from them.
Penn. v. Bornman, 1882, 26 Albany L. J. 232, and Workingmens Banking
Co. v. Rantenberg, 102 Ill. 523; 26 Albany L. J. 475.   A church was held
not capable of contracting for a steamboat excursion for the purpose of
raising money to pay the church debt, consequently it could not recover
damages for breach of such contract.   Harriman v. First etc. Church,
63 Ga. 186; Am. L. Rev., 1883, p. 206.
[2] National Mutual Aid Association v. Lupold, Pa., 1882, 15 C. L. N.
278.

many go even so far as to establish tribunals for the adjusting of private controversies between member and member. It becomes, therefore, of interest to ascertain what relation such society tribunals bear to the ordinary courts of the State.

Furthermore, as many of these bodies are unincorporated (and, therefore, not subject to the ordinary rules governing corporations), and as they can not be regarded as individuals or co-partnerships, they may appear to have no especial legal status at all, and thus not at all subject to being brought into court; a perusal of the following pages will, however, show the manner in which they are subjected to litigation.

Further cases, in which the relation of the courts of the State towards the tribunals of the societies is considered, will be found where the expulsion of members is treated of.

§ 11. **How and When Subjected to Litigation.**— As stated above, when these bodies are incorporated, litigation by or against them would be conducted under the statutes of the State relating to incorporations, but when they are not incorporated various forms of procedure have been announced, upon which matter the following cases are collated.

An early English case [1] concerned the "Amicable Society of Master Bakers." In the course of the argument, Sir Samuel Romilly said : "Societies of this nature are much favored, and are considered as peculiarly under the protection of the legislature and of courts of justice."[2] The case was decided by Lord ELDON, who ordered a calculation to be made to see whether the funds would be sufficient to pay the annuities claimed in the suit against the societies as

[1] Pearce v. Piper, 17 Vesey, 19, 1809.
[2] Still there did not appear to be any particular act of Parliament involved in the case. Very elaborate Statutes, said to be modeled after the Imperial Statutes, can be found in New Zealand, Victoria, New South Wales, South Australia, and Tasmania (there are probably still others). These are called "Friendly Society Acts," and regulate to the utmost detail the nature of the business, membership, risks, reports, accounts, etc., of these beneficiary associations.

also those which would soon be claimed, and he decided
that if the fund proved insufficient he would re-arrange the
system, or, if nothing else could be done, would dissolve
the society.[1]

The principle upon which the interference of the courts
may be expected to be obtained is stated as follows : " With
these voluntary associations the court, before it interferes,
must see that it is under obligations to act, and that it can
effectually act for the benefit of the persons who have laid
out their money in a way in which there must be so much
difficulty in recovering it." [2] Where there are no property
rights, the courts will not interfere at all.[3]

A court of equity will protect the rights of members of
an unincorporated " Fire Society," and will restrain any
disposition of the funds different from the manner and purposes declared in the rules of the society.[4] And will compel the transfer of funds from former trustees to new trustees of a " Pressmen's Union," an unincorporated association formed for securing a fair system of labor and
charitable assistance to members.[5] So where an association
had been formed to free a district from the war draft, by
furnishing substitutes, it was held that a surplus fund remaining could not, except by unanimous consent, be turned
over to a charitable institution, and a court of equity would
prevent this being done.[6]

A club had been formed for the mutual insurance of the
ships of the members. The plaintiff having lost his vessel
brought suit against the secretary and treasurer and seven
members,[7] alleging that the members were too numerous to

---

[1] See also, Reeve v. Parkins, 2 Jac. & Walk. 390.
[2] Ellison v. Bignold, 2 Jacob & Walkers, 503.
[3] Rigby v. Connell, 28 W. R. 650; 11 Cent. L. J., 19.
[4] Torrey v. Baker, 1 Allen, Mass. 120.
[5] Birmingham v. Gallagher, 112 Mass. 190.
[6] Abels v. McKeen, 18 N. J. Eq., 462. And will give each member his
share. Foley v. Tovey, 54 Pa. St. 190.
[7] The number seven was fixed upon evidently on account of its supposed cabalistic virtues; there does not appear to have been any statute
directing the form of suit.

be all brought into court; and he asked that payment be ordered to be made to him from the funds of the association, and if these were not sufficient, that a ratable contribution be made from all who were members at the time when he joined the club. The defendants demurred, and stated that the plaintiff could not thus sue, but it was decided that the suit was brought in proper form.[1]

A court will enjoin the circulation of libelous articles directed against a friendly society and injurious to its business interests.[2]

In New York the statute which allows unincorporated associations to sue in the name of their treasurers, was held to apply to Sons of Temperance.[3]

But under this statute its form must be strictly followed, and thus whilst plaintiff could have properly sued the Unterstuetzungs Verein by a suit directed against its president or treasurer, yet it was held that his suit against the president, treasurer and secretary was improperly brought.[4]

And a court will not entertain a suit in the name of an unincorporated association, especially when it has been formed for the purpose of resisting the (liquor) laws. The State would not incorporate or sanction a society whose object is to resist the very laws of the State itself, and hence such society, when unincorporated, can certainly not sue in a corporate name.[5]

Plaintiff cannot, in his own name, sue " for the benefit of the National Loan Fund Life Assurance Society " (unincorporated), nor can he, in such a case, do so by averring that the other parties are so numerous that it is impracticable to bring them all before the court; in order to go upon this theory, the common interest of all parties must be such that each, if before the court, could maintain the same action

[1] Bromley v. Williams. 32 Beav. 177.
[2] Hill v. Hart, 47 L. T. R. (N. S.) 82.
[3] Tibbits v. Blood, 21 Barb. 650.
[4] Schmidt v. Gunther, 5 Daly, 452.
[5] Detroit Schuetzenbund v. Detroit Agitations Verein, 44 Mich. 313 s. c., 38 Am. R. 270.

in his own name and in his own right. But the general agent of such society may maintain such suit, as also could plaintiff if he satisfactorily shows special authorization from the society.[1]

The statute which authorizes suits against associations concerning their "joint property and effects," was held not to apply to the unincorporated Mining Stock Board on a question of membership, and, therefore, an injunction suit directed (according to said statute) against the president, was not to be considered a suit against the whole association.[2]

A court of equity will not dissolve an unincorporated Hose Company and distribute the funds among the members, so long as there are those who are ready to execute the public trust with which the fund has been clothed.[3]

A cornet band had a rule that any member withdrawing, "leaves all his interest with the band." Held, that the remaining members could maintain the action of trover against one who left and took his cornet with him.[4]

While it is decided that an action at law would not lie against one member of a yacht club, in favor of the others, for damages sustained in his building a defective yacht for the club, it is strongly intimated that a suit in equity would have been proper.[5]

The members of the Community of which George Rapp was patriarch, were held to be to some extent under religious duress, therefore the court set aside a receipt in full obtained from an expelled member, as being not voluntarily given, and interfered in his behalf and maintained his claim for a share of the common property, although under the rules of the association he was not entitled thereto.[6]

---

[1] Habicht v. Pemberton, 4 Sandf. (N. Y.) 657.

[2] Rorke v. Russell, 2 Lans. (N. Y.) 244.

[3] Thomas v. Ellmaker, 1 Parson's Select Cases (Pa.) 98. This case has very full arguments and opinion.

[4] Danbury Cornet Band v. Bean, 54 N. H. 524.

[5] McMahon v. Rauhr, 47 N. Y. 67.

[6] Nachtrieb v. The Harmony Settlement, 3 Wallace, Jr. 66. But see somewhat similar case where relief was not given, Grosvenor v. United,

A note was payable to "the treasurer of the Tuskaloosa Jockey Club" (unincorporated); this could not be sued upon by the treasurer. Had it been payable to him in his own name, and describing him as treasurer, then such description could have been disregarded, and he in his own name would have been considered as a trustee for the other members, and could have brought suit.[1]

The colored people had arranged a fair, and after the same had been for some time in successful progress, certain self-appointed trustees obtaining possession of the fund which the fair produced, were about to devote the same to a purpose different from that originally contemplated; but they were enjoined from doing this, upon a bill filed by one of the original promotors of the fair.[2] And a similar interference by a court of equity was made in behalf of an evangelical society which had acquired, by contributions, etc., a fund to be used in aiding young men to obtain a christian education.[3]

Members of a voluntary unincorporated association may sue at law or in equity in their own names : so held in a case allowing the members of the "Southern Orphans Association" to maintain, in equity, their right to a disputed fund.[4]

While an unincorporated lodge of Free Masons could not sue as a corporation, for the delivery of chattels, yet Lord Eldon allowed them to amend their pleading and sue as individuals, for the delivery of hall decorations wrongfully withheld by the defendant.[5] And so the defendant was or-

etc. (Shakers), 118 Mass. 78, in which the court refused to interfere with the determination made by the officials of the "Shakers" upon the question of their religious tenets, deciding as to who were, and who were not, entitled to membership in the Community. The Shakers compact was also held valid in Waite v. Merrill, 4 Me. (4 Greenl.) 102, deciding that a departing member has no claim for wages.

[1] Ewing v. Medlock, 5 Porter (Ala.) 82.
[2] Morton v. Smith, 5 Bush. Ky. 469.
[3] Penfield v. Skinner, 11 Vt. 296.
[4] Mears v. Moulton, 30 Md. 142.
[5] Lloyd v. Loaring, 9 Vesey, Jr. 773. See, also, Smith v. Smith, 3 Desau., (S. C.), 557.

dered, on the suit of the other members, to deliver to the
proper club officer, the silver tobacco box which such officer
had the privilege and duty of keeping.[1]

The Connecticut Statute which allowed suit against persons associated without corporate power, but with distinguishing name, to be in such name, was held to apply also
to a militia company.[2]

The members of an unincorporated association should not
sue as a corporation, but should sue as if they were partners.[3]

There are cases, however, in which the courts will disre-
gard the entire machinery of these unincorporated bodies,
as having no legal status at all. A very good illustration,
which will be given here at some length, is found in a case
concerning an Odd Fellows lodge. The plaintiff, as treasurer of Cayuga Lodge, sued the defendants for certain
lodge property, and stated that the defendants had formerly
constituted said lodge, but had been expelled by the Grand
Lodge, and their charter revoked, and that plaintiffs had
then been installed by the Grand Lodge, as constituting
said Cayuga Lodge, and had been directed to receive from
the defendants all the lodge property. The court,[4] however, decided (on demurrer) that plaintiffs in the above
statements, had failed to show themselves entitled to the
property, because if they were, it would follow that the
vast property accumulated by the many lodges, would be
under absolute control of the Grand Lodge, which again
would be under control of the National Grand Lodge, and
continued: "This is entirely unobjectionable so long as
submission to these (lodge) decrees is merely voluntary;
but the question is, whether that submission is to be legally

[1] Fells v. Read, 3 Vesey, Jr. 30.
[2] Fox v. Narramore, 36 Conn. 382.
[3] Pipe v. Bateman, 1 Iowa, 369. This decision, however, relates to an
association formed with a view to pecuniary profit, and, as stated in the
introductory remarks, the rules laid down as to such cannot be deemed
entirely applicable to the other association. This case gives a number
of English cases.
[4] Austin v. Searing, 16 N. Y. 112.

and judicially enforced." * * * * * "Were it distinctly averred that the defendants had subscribed the constitution of the Grand, as well as of the subordinate Lodge,
I would still be of the opinion that public policy would not
admit of parties binding themselves by such engagements."
* * * .* "To create a judicial tribunal is one of the
functions of the sovereign power." Consequently, it was
unanimously decided that the defendants were not bound
by the decree rendered against them in the Grand Lodge,
and that such decree formed no valid basis on which to rest
the law suit.

It would seem that the real theory of the last decision is
not so much upon the fact that the lodge was an unincorporated body, as it is upon the consideration of the public
policy of not allowing too much power to rest in the hands of
these bodies. In a more recent case,[1] the Supreme Lodge
of A. O. U. W., incorporated under the laws of Kentucky,
demanded assessments of the Michigan Grand Lodge, which
in turn demanded them from the members of subordinate
lodges, but it was decided by the courts, that this could not
be done. "It is not competent for the respondent (the
Grand Lodge) to subject itself or its members, to a foreign
authority in this way. There is no law of the State per-
mitting it, nor could there be any law of the State which
would subject a corporation created and existing under the
laws of this State, to the jurisdiction and control of a body
existing in another State and in no manner under control of
our laws."

And it has also been decided that the Grand Lodge of
Pennsylvania A. O. U. W., had no power to demand assessments from members of subordinate lodges, in order to
raise a fund to be sent to the other States, because by its
charter it (the Grand Lodge) is limited to the relief of the
members of its own lodge, and of its subordinate lodges.[2]

---

[1] Lamphere v. Grand Lodge A. O. U. W., 47 Mich. Also 11 N. W. R. 268.

[2] Corona Lodge v. Grand Lodge, decision by Judge Stowe, reported in
"Iowa Workman," April 15, 1883. This is one of the "Relief Fund"
cases, and similar cases are now pending in Iowa.

The majority of the Teutonia Lodge D. O. H. (an unincorporated benevolent association) withdrew, and surrendered their charter to the Grand Lodge, and formed a new lodge. The minority, remaining, then received the charter from the Grand Lodge, and the court decided that they were entitled to recover the lodge property from the body composed by the others, viz., the majority.[1]

The majority of a Good Templars lodge refused to pay a certain tax to the Grand Lodge; the minority withdrew and paid the tax, and had their officials installed by the Grand Lodge as representing the original lodge, they then sued the majority for the lodge property. Their bill was dismissed by the court, on the ground that the Grand Lodge had not as yet declared forfeited the charter under which the majority branch still claimed to act, and because, further, the plaintiffs had not applied for relief to the Grand Lodge itself; the court refusing relief until every means offered in the Order itself should have been tried.[2]

The court entertained a bill in equity to decide as to which of different officials of the (unincorporated) "Knights of St. Crispin," were entitled to the possession of certain funds.[3]

Probably one of the most interesting cases, certainly to Masons, is *Smith* v. *Smith.*[4] In this the history of the Ancient York Masons and of the Free and Accepted Masons, is very elaborately reviewed, and it was held that a union of the grand lodges of these two was not valid as against subordinate lodges objecting thereto, and that these objecting lodges having themselves formed a grand lodge, constituted the genuine one, and were entitled to the lodge funds.

The foregoing pages, particularly at commencement of chapter, have shown that the courts will interfere for the

---

[1] Altman v. Berry, 27 N. J. Eq., 331.

[2] Chamberlain v. Lincoln, 129 Mass. 70.

[3] Snow v. Wheeler, 113 Mass. 179; also deciding that the society was not rendered illegal by one of its rules, which prohibited members from teaching their trade to others, except with the society's consent.

[4] 2 Desau., (S. C.) 557.

purpose of protecting property rights of members of unincorporated associations, and when they do interfere, it may be stated with safety, that the rules which the courts will follow, are essentially the same as those rules which guide the courts when dealing with formally incorporated bodies of the same kind. The following cases, dealing mostly with regularly incorporated bodies, are of interest in showing the relation between State tribunals and lodge or society tribunals, and the importance which is attached to the latter; as once before remarked, still other cases will be found later in this book when discussing the topic of expulsion of members.

A report was made by an Odd Fellows' committee, in which, on the question of expulsion from the lodge, they stated that a member had been guilty of perjury. It was decided that this would not give to him a right of action against the members of the committee for damages as for libel, unless the report was made with malice. It was said that the report was to be considered as a privileged communication.[1]

Concerning Washington Tent No. 1, of the Independent Order of Rechabites, the court decided[2] that it would not order a dissolution of the same, on account of hostility and irreconcilable differences among factions of the members, so long as the existing grievances could be righted by appeals to the higher powers in the Order, and no attempt had been made to take such appeal, saying: "courts should not, as a general rule, interfere with the contentions and quarrels of voluntary associations, so long as the government is fairly and honestly administered, and those who have grievances should be required in the first instance to resort to remedies for redress provided by their rules and regulations."

[1] Kirkpatrick v. Eagle Lodge, 26 Kansas, 384; also 40 Am. R. 316. A full discussion of the matter of privileged communications can be found in Shurtleff v. Stevens, 51 Vt. 501, given with valuable notes in 31 Am. R. 698.

[2] Lafond v. Deems, 81 N. Y. 507. See also Fischer v. Raab, 57 How Pr. 87.

The charter and laws of the Order of Red Men required that any member claiming his benefits, if refused by his lodge, should appeal to Grand Tribe, first of the State, and then of the United States. Plaintiff went through these steps, but the Grand Tribe of the State, and then of the United States, decided against him. Afterward he sued in the State court for his benefits, and was awarded them by the lower court, but this was reversed in the Supreme Court,[1] upon the ground that the decision in the tribunals of the order is binding upon the courts of the State, saying: "These are private beneficial institutions operating on the members only, who, for reasons of policy and convenience affecting their welfare, and, perhaps, their existence, adopt laws for their government to be administered by themselves, to which every person who joins them assents. They require the surrender of no right that a man may not waive, and are obligatory on him only so long as he chooses to recognize their authority. In the present instance, the party appears to have been subjected to the general laws and by-laws according to the usual course, and if the tribunal of his own choice has decided against him, he ought not to complain. It would very much impair the usefulness of such institutions if they are to be harrassed by petty suits of this kind, and this probably was a controlling consideration in determining the manner of assessing benefits and passing upon the conduct of members."

In another suit,[2] against this same Order, for benefits, the point was made in the argument that the court could have no jurisdiction, but it was answered by the opposing counsel by saying that there was nothing in the constitution denying the right to sue. The court does not appear to have decided this question directly, but it did entertain the suit, and left it for the jury to decide whether the deceased was in arrears or not.

[1] Osceola Tribe v. Schmidt, 57 Maryland, 98; 25 Albany L. J. 333, citing Anacosta, etc. v. Murbach, 13 Maryland, 94. See also, Black, etc. v. Vandyke, 2 Wharton, 309.

[2] Logan Tribe v. Schwartz, 19 Md. 565.

Even if a member would otherwise be heard in the State tribunals, yet he must first exhaust all the appeals and remedies given within the Order or Association itself.[1]

The benefit being payable " whilst so much remained in the funds," it was decided that a member could not sue in the courts for his benefit, as the courts would presume that the corporation had determined that there was not so much in the funds, and such determination would be conclusive upon the courts.[2]

An incorporated lodge of Odd Fellows may determine who are not members, and the courts will leave this to the rules and judicial officers of the lodge, regardless whether the charter does or does not, in express terms, give such powers to these officers.[3]

Where, however, there has been no agreement that disputes should be referred to any tribunal within the Order possessing conclusive jurisdiction, a member may sue at law for his weekly allowances.[4]

But in another case it is said the society never intended to be subjected to such petty and vexatious suits, and that the proper remedy is mandamus for reinstatement.[5]

A medical society threatened to expel a member who harbored the homeopathic heresy. He applied to the courts for an injunction to prevent this being done, but the same was refused. The court declined to prevent the judicial officers of the society from passing upon the accusation ; it was said that such officers are, to that extent, a court, and that a court of chancery is not the proper tribunal to correct the errors and irregularities of such other court.[6]

[1] Harrington v. Workingmens Benevolent Association, Ga. 1883, 27 Albany L. J. 438. See also Olery v. Brown, 51 How. Pr. 92; White v. Brownell, 2 Daly, 329; 3 Ab. Pr. (N. S.) 318; 4 Id. 162, especially 4, 199; Chamberlain v. Lincoln, *supra*, page 46.

[2] Toram v. The Howard Beneficial Association, 4 Pa. St. 519.

[3] State, *rel.*, Poulson v. Odd Fellows, 8 Mo. App. 148.

[4] Dolan v. Court Good Samaritan A. O. Foresters, 128 Mass. 437. See also Smith v. Society, 12 Phila. (Pa.) 380; Cartan v. The Father Matthews U. B. S., 3 Daly (N. Y.), 20.

[5] Black etc. v. Vandyke, 2 Wharton, 309.

[6] Gregg v. Mass. Medical Society, 111 Mass. 185; *s. c.*, 15 Am. R. 24.

But the courts will not be bound by decisions made by the officials of an Order concerning the force and effect of its contracts. Thus where witnesses were called to prove that it was the custom to make payments only in lodge meetings, and to prove that the officials of the Order had decided that it was necessary to do so, the court *refused* to hear any such evidence, and construed the contract according to the written terms, and decided that payment to the financier outside of the lodge was sufficient.[1]

§ 12. **Expulsion of Members.**—As was stated in a former section, the cases on the expulsion of members will present, in many instances, the question of how far and under what circumstances the courts will interfere in the conduct of these societies and associations. It need not be said that this topic of expulsion of members is a very important one ; by this act the member is deprived of insurance to which he may have contributed for many years ; his family may suffer for much needed assistance in times of sickness, and, indeed, there may be the loss of a considerable value in real or personal property attending the expulsion. In this view it must certainly be admitted that to expel a member is to deprive him of property rights, and, consequently, that the courts will be open to hear his complaint and give appropriate redress if the expulsion be improper.

The cases here given will show the principles which guide the courts in determining questions of this sort.

Whilst most of the decisions which follow relate to formally incorporated bodies, yet there is no reason why the principles laid down should not apply to those which are unincorporated ; we have seen in a former section that these also are favorably regarded by the courts, and all property rights of members jealously protected. A recent English case[2] tends to prove that the courts are fully as considerate in dealing with the unincorporated as with the others. The case relates to an unincorporated mutual

---

[1] Manson v. Grand Lodge A. O. U. W. Minn., 16 N. W. R. 395.

[2] Wood v. Woad, L. R. 9 Exch. 190; 10 Eng. R. (Moak.) 372.

marine insurance society, and it was decided that a member could not be expelled without notice of the charge against him, and opportunity to defend himself, although the rules of the society expressly stated that a member could be expelled at any time that the committee deemed his conduct suspicious, in which case it (the committee) was simply to direct the secretary to give such member " notice in writing that the committee have excluded such member from the society." The language of the decision is so apt that an extensive extract is here given :

" This then is the great question in the case : Was the alleged act of expulsion void? It is contended for the plaintiff, that the language of the rules gives an unconditional and absolute power to the committee to expel a member from the society, and I agree that if the committee, in fact, exercised their power under the rules, their decision could not be questioned ; however unfounded the reasons for it may have been, it would have been final, and could not be reviewed by any court. But they are bound in the exercise of their functions by the rule expressed in the maxim, *audi alteram partem*, that no man shall be condemned to consequences resulting from alleged misconduct unheard, and without having the opportunity of making his defence. This rule is not confined to the conduct of strictly legal tribunals, but is applicable to every tribunal or body of persons invested with authority to adjudicate upon matters involving civil consequences to individuals." [1]

Where property interests are involved, as where a club owned considerable property, and where the club was formally incorporated, it was said that a member could not be expelled unless the power of expulsion be expressly conferred by the charter ; with this exception, however, that the club had the implied power of expelling a member who had been convicted of an infamous crime, or who had been guilty of some act against the society tending to its injury

[1] For the purposes of this case the association was treated as a partnership, but that it is not such, see pages referred to in Index, under Partnership.

or destruction.[1] And so it was said, furthermore, that a by-law under which expulsion was ordered for minor offences was void ; consequently the court reinstated the plaintiff as a member, he having been expelled for striking another member whilst in the club rooms.

The distinction between expulsion and amotion must not be overlooked ; the latter merely means to remove an officer from his office, without expelling him, and if he is subject to removal on a "reasonable cause," and this has been done, the court will not at all interfere, unless perhaps in cases in which the proceedings were fraudulently conducted ;[2] in other cases the corporation is the only judge of what constitutes reasonable cause for amotion, and the courts will abide by its decision.

The courts do not, however, regard with great favor, the assumption of too much power on the part of any corporation or association. Thus the Butchers Beneficial Association[3] applied, under the statute, to the court for the purpose of obtaining a charter, in which, among others, the power was granted to expel "any member guilty of actions which may injure the Association." The court refused to comply with the request, upon the ground that this might include the expulsion of a member simply for becoming insolvent, and said: "It is totally incompatible with the whole spirit of our institutions, to clothe any body with such indefinite power over the members, for it is an equivalent to socialism and a rejection of all individual rights within the Association."

Again, where the power of expelling for "improper conduct" was given, as also the power of "adjusting controversies between members," and the controversy related to a question for determining which no provision had been

---

[1] Evans v. Philadelphia Club, 50 Pa. 107 (14 Wright). This is a very instructive case, with exhaustive arguments and opinion. The lower court decided for the plaintiff, and the Supreme Court, on an even division, sustained the decision. See also, for grounds of expulsion, People, rel., Bartlet v. Medical Society, 32 N. Y. 194.

[2] Inderwick v. Snell, 2 Macnaghton & Gordon, 216.

[3] 11 Casey, (Pa.) 151.

made, it was decided by the court that a member could not
be expelled for refusing to obey a decision made by the
Exchange Tribunal.[1]

The incorporated St. Patrick's Benevolent Society, had
a by-law which made it an offence, subject to expulsion, for
one member to "vilify" another. But the court reinstated
a member who had been expelled for violating this by-law;
and did so upon the ground that such a law was not necessary for the good government and support of the corporation,[2] and said: "The right of membership is valuable, and
is not to be taken away without an authority fairly derived
either from the charter or the nature of corporate bodies."
* * * * * "The offence of vilifying a member, or a
private quarrel, is totally unconnected with the affairs of
the society, and therefore its punishment cannot be necessary for the good government of the corporation. So far
from it, that it appears to me, that taking cognizance of
such offences, will have the pernicious effect of introducing
private feuds into the bosom of the society, and interrupt-
ing the transaction of business."

The courts will not sustain a by-law, although it be in
conformity with the charter, if it is against the common law.
The by-law of an Exchange provided for the expulsion of
any member who sued another at law, without first having
offered to submit to arbitrators in the Exchange. The
court held[3] such by-law unreasonable, and that a member,
who had, indeed, submitted to an arbitration, but had then
refused compliance and been expelled, should be re-instated.
The court went upon the theory that merchants were under
some sort of compulsion to join the Exchange, for any one
not joining would be at a great disadvantage in business
matters, as in the Exchange nearly all the business was
done. Therefore, a member being thus forced to join,
should not be deprived of his legal rights of suing others,

[1] People v. Cotton Exchange, 8 Hun. (15 N. Y. S. C.), 216.

[2] Commonwealth v. St. P. B. S., 2 Binney 448.

[3] State rel. Kennedy v. Union Merchants' Exchange, St. Louis Court
of Appeals (1876), 3 Central L. J. 290.

especially not by an arbitration, for arbitrators frequently act erroneously, and still there would be no appeal from their decision.

But in another Board of Trade case,[1] these bodies were said to be mere voluntary associations, although incorporated, and on the same footing as masonic, and such other bodies; the Board "is not engaged in business, but only prescribes rules for the transaction of business," consequently the courts will not re-instate expelled members. It was also said that in the earlier case,[2] this question had not been raised at all.

It has been said that the courts will interfere where property rights are involved; but where there are none, the courts will not interfere at all. Thus a member was refused reinstatement to a Trades Union, partly because its object seemed to be in restraint of trade, hence illegal, but more particularly because he did not allege that the Union possessed any property. The learned Sir George Jessel, M. R., said : "No court of justice can interfere so long as there is no property, the rights to which are taken away from the person complaining."[3] He illustrates by supposing a whist club, and some members refusing to play with others, of course the courts would not interfere, and he distinguishes cases in which property rights were involved.[4]

If a member is expelled, the courts will not review the merits of the case, but will consider the society as the sole judge. It was declared an offence for a member to be engaged in his usual business or "occupation" whilst drawing the benefits accruing during sickness. The plaintiff, whilst too sick to work, painted the handle to the gate at his home ; being expelled for this, he was reinstated by the trial court, but the Supreme Court reversed the decision, saying : "The

---

[1] People rel. Rice v. Board of Trade of Chicago, 80 Ill. 134.
[2] Page v. Board of Trade, 45 Ill. 112.
[3] Rigby v. Connell, 28 W. R. 650; 11 Central L. J. 19.
[4] St. James Club, 13 Eng. L. & E. 589; 2 De G. M. & G. 387; Hopkinson v. Marquis, 16 W. R. 266; L. R. 5 Eq. Cas. 66, 63.

society acted judicially, and its sentence is conclusive like that of any other ·judicial tribunal.'' [1]

The courts will, however, decide whether the ground for expulsion is well taken ; thus a member was expelled for not paying the award found due by the arbitrators, his conduct being declared to amount to a '' wilful violation of the constitution and by-laws.'' But the court (finding that the member had honestly supposed that the arbitrators had acted without jurisdiction), decided that he could not be deemed guilty of any *wilful* violation ; also that the arbitration itself could be reviewed in the courts the same as any other arbitration,[2] and that the only effect of disobeying it, was to subject the members to a law suit thereon. As a contrast to this, may be read the admission of the counsel in another case,[3] he being of the view that such an award could not be made the basis of a law suit, and that the member refusing to obey it could be expelled. This case gives a very extensive discussion of the jurisdiction of the '' Open Board of Stock Brokers '' over its members ; it is almost a complete work upon these topics, and comes to the conclusion that the only questions which can arise are, whether the expulsion was in accordance with the rules, whether the same were in accordance with the law of the land, and that the courts will only interfere in order to hold these bodies to a fair and honest administration of their rules.[4] But where there is no method provided in the internal machinery of the association for correcting injustice to a member, there the courts will interfere.[5]

[1] Commonwealth v. Pike Beneficial Society, 8 W. & S. (Pa.) 250; also Black, etc. v. Vandyke, 2 Wharton, 309; Burt v. Grand Lodge F. and A. M. 44 Mich. 208; Robinson v. Yates City Lodge, 86 Ill. 598.

[2] Savannah Cotton Exchange v. State, 54 Ga. 668.

[3] White v. Brownell, 4 Ab. Pr. (N. s.) 183. But if a member resigns, that revokes his agreement to submit to arbitration, and any thereafter made is invalid. Heath v. N. Y. Gold Exch., 38 How. Pr. 171. That arbitration can not be compelled, see State v. Chamber of Commerce, 20 Wis. 63.

[4] This case occurs in following places: 2 Daly (N. Y.) 329; 3 Ab. Pr. (N. s.) 318; 4 Id. 162. But see to contrary, State, *rel.* Kennedy v. Union Mchts. Ex., St. Louis Court of Appeals, 1876, 3 Central L. J. 290

[5] Olery v. Brown, 51 How. Pr. 92.

In reference to an expelled member of a club, the rules were laid down that the courts have no right to interfere with decisions of clubs in regard to their members, except in the following cases: First, if the decision arrived at was contrary to natural justice, such as the member complained of not having an opportunity to explain misconduct; secondly, if the rules of the club had not been observed; thirdly, if the action of the club was malicious, and not *bona fide*.[1]

The courts will not even review cases in which the proceedings are not strictly according to the rules, if no substantial rights were affected.[2]

A member of a Board of Trade having been expelled, his right to reinstatement must be tried at law, and until thus settled, a court of equity will not interfere by injunction to restore him to his position, even though he may, in the meantime, suffer a loss of profits.[3]

While mandamus is a proper proceedure to be invoked by an expelled member,[4] especially when no objection is made thereto, yet it is said that the better way would be for the injured party to pursue his remedy in a common law suit.[5]

If a member recovers damages for his wrongful expulsion, he cannot afterward claim to be reinstated.[6]

An expulsion, though illegal if acquiesced in for a long time (e. g., nineteen years), can not then be reviewed in the courts, at least not unless good excuse for the delay is shown.[7]

[1] Dawkins v. Autrobus, 44 L. T. Rep. (N. S.) 557; 24 Albany L. J. 138. Also Lambert v. Addison, 46 L. T. Rep. (N. S.) 20; 25 Albany L. J. 418; Gardner v. Freemantel, 24 L. T. 81; 19 W. R. 256.

[2] Burton v. St. George Society, 28 Mich 261.

[3] Sturges v. Chicago B. of T. 86 Ill. 441; Baxter v. B. of T. 83 Ill. 146.

[4] Doyle v. New York, etc., 6 Th. & C. 85; s. c., 3 Hun. 360; O'Reily v. Mutual L. I. Co., 2 Abb. Pr. (N. Y.) N. S. 167; State v. Chamber of Commerce, 20 Wis. 63. See also pages referred to in Index, under mandamus.

[5] Lamphire v. Grand Lodge A. O. U. W. 47 Mich. 11 N. W. R. 268.

[6] State, *rel*, Kloppstein v. Slavonska Lipa, 28 Ohio St. 665.

[7] Bostwick v. Fire Department, 14 N. W. R. 501.

§ 13. **Proceedings in Expulsion.**— They must be in every respect regular, as has already been seen, and the facts must be sufficient. A member having brought mandamus for reinstatement, it was decided that the society did not make a sufficient return (defence) in merely stating that he had been expelled for defrauding the society, but that it should have set forth the facts in full, and that the society records should contain them in full, and that these facts must show that there was fraud; as this had not been done, the member was reinstated.[1]

And where a member had been expelled for "slander" against the society, he was reinstated because the records failed to show the facts, and because there should have been shown such words, uttered by him, as would, at least, have been analogous to words which constitute the common law offence of slander.[2] The facts must be set forth distinctly and certainly, not argumentatively, inferentially or evasively, and must sufficiently show the cause of the expulsion and the mode of the proceeding.[3]

A physician was expelled from a medical society upon the ground that he had ceased to be, as required, a "gentleman of respectable social position." His offence consisted in going upon the bail bond of some colored prisoners, and upon the official bonds of other colored men. The court reinstated him.[4]

The member is entitled to a trial before the entire society, and can not be put on trial before a committee.[5]

[1] Commonwealth, *rel.* Fischer v. The German Society, 15 Pa. St. 251.
[2] Roehler v. The Mechanics Aid Society, 22 Mich. 86.
[3] Society for Visitation of the Sick v. Meyer, 52 Pa. St. 125.
[4] State *rel.* Waring v. The Georgia Medical Society, 38 Ga. 608. The arguments and the opinion are very elaborate in this case. There is also a valuable note (when case was below) in 8 Am. Law Register, 537.
[5] (Of course if such committee is expressly provided for, then he can be validly tried before it). On the above point see Commonwealth, *rel.* Fischer v. The German Society, 15 Pa. St. 251; also Green v. African M. E. S., 1 S. & R. 254. The power of amotion (probably court meant expulsion) and suspension can not be delegated to the board of directors. State v. Chamber of Commerce, 20 Wisc. 63. The Grand Chancellor K. of P. can not suspend an officer of the grand or subordinate

The expulsion must be by formal act. In a case in which
the rule was that if any member " neglect to pay his arrear-
ages for three months, he shall be expelled," it was held
that it was not sufficient to merely drop him from the list,
but that there would have to be a formal vote of expulsion.[1]

The majority of a Good Templars lodge refused to pay a
certain Grand Lodge tax ; the minority then withdrew,
formed a new lodge, and the Grand Lodge installed its
officers ; but the court held that this did not amount to an
expulsion of the majority branch, nor to a revocation of the
charter which they still held, and that the formal vote and
act of revocation in the Grand Lodge was necessary to
effect this.[2]

Before he can be expelled he must have notice of the
charges against him and an opportunity to defend himself,
(i. e., a trial) because before he can be expelled for being
in arrears, the court says,[3] " it may be that he may either
prove that he is not in arrears or give such reason for his
default as the society may think sufficient."[4] When a
member is entitled to notice of being in arrears, it is not
competent to leave it to the secretary to declare a forfeiture
for non-payment, as this is making the secretary both wit-
ness and judge, without hearing or appeal, in a matter de-
pending on his own performance of a prior duty.[5] The

lodge, without trial and judgment by the lodge. Lowry v. Stotzer, 7
Phila. 397.
  [1] Commonwealth v. The Pennsylvania B. I. 2 S. & R. 141. See also,
State v. Cartaret, 40 N. J. L. 295.
  [2] Chamberlain v. Lincoln, 129 Mass. 70.
  [3] In Comm. v. The Pennsylvania, etc., 2 S. & R. 141. See also that notice
is necessary. Doyle v. New York, etc., 6 Th. & C. 85 s. c. 3 Hun. 360.
  [4] If it be distinctly provided that a member in arrears may be expelled
or simply dropped, without notice, he may then be thus expelled or
dropped. See Madeira v. Merchant, etc. Society, C. C. E. D., Mo. 16,
F. R. 749.
  For expulsion without notice, policy being void by mere failure to
pay, see Illinois Masonic, etc. v. Baldwin, 77 Ill. 479. For an instance
in which notice of dues was held necessary, according to the rules of the
association, see Mutual Endowment Assessment Association v. Essender,
(59 Md. 463,) 28 Albany L. J. 80.
  [5] Pulford v. Detroit Fire Department, 31 Mich. 458.

notice should be given personally,[1] (unless some other mode
has been agreed upon). This was a very strong case, and
the society was held bound to notify the member, although
he had changed his residence without giving in the new ad-
dress (for this omission he was, however, under another
rule, subject to a fine). This rule of notice is an important one; the courts will be very slow to sustain an expulsion not founded on notice. In an army and navy club in
which the by-laws allowed *immediate expulsion*, where the
offence was of so grave a character as to warrant the same,
it was decided that a member who had been thus expelled
for having called a guest of the club a liar, should be reinstated[2] for the purpose of receiving notice of the accusation, and defending himself on trial.[3]

If the expulsion be without notice, the courts will interfere, although the rules may not provide for the giving of
notice.[4]

If the facts clearly set forth sufficiently show an offence,
the courts will of course not disturb the judgment of the
society tribunal, as for instance upon the charge of scandal-

[1] Wachtel v. Noah Widows and O. S., 84 N. Y. 28, also in 38 Am. R.
478. The notice should be specific; it will not do to state that meeting
is "to take into consideration the conduct of" a member. Examine
Cannon v. Toronto Corn Ex., 27 Grants (U. C.) Chy. 23. Labouchere v.
Wharncliffe, 13 Ch., D. L. R. 246.

[2] Fisher v. Kean, 41 L. T. (N. S.) 335; 27 English Reports (Moak)
586.

[3] The theory of the case is that the offence was not of so grave a character as to warrant immediate expulsion, hence the expulsion could only
be in the usual manner, that is on notice and trial. It would be difficult to sustain any expulsion not founded on notice, though the rules
should distinctly provide for the same. Courts are loath to have parties
deprived of rights without an opportunity to defend them. This would
especially be true in matters of a personal nature, as for instance expelling on account of offences committed; but it is very common to provide for expulsion, without notice, for non-payment of dues. This is
valid; and it would be almost impossible to carry on an insurance plan
in any other manner. Indeed it has been held that notice need not be
given although there was a custom of giving it. See Mutual Fire Ins.
Co. v. Miller Lodge, 58 Maryland, 463; Thompson v. Knickerbocker Life
Ins. Co. 104, U. S. 252, both stated in this book, pp. 32-33.

[4] Fritz v. Much, 62 How. Pr. 69.

ous and improper proceedings injurious to the society, a member was proven to have raised his physician's bill from $4 to $40 ; for this he was held properly expelled.[1]

Expulsion is not necessarily confined to the same rules as litigation would be. Thus, although an *unwritten* contract may be void by the statute of a State, yet a member of a Chamber of Commerce was held to have been properly expelled for failing to comply with such a contract, as according to the rules, he should have done. The court found that as there was nothing illegal or immoral in contracts (merely because they are not written), and as the object of the corporation was " to personate just and equitable principles of trade," it was certainly proper to compel a member to perform his contract, though unwritten and not enforceable in the courts.[2]

Members of an incorporated association cannot be expelled for the violation of a mere by-law, unless the expulsion therefor is allowed by the Statutes or charter of incorporation.[3]

§ 14. **Concerning Admission.**— Naturally there is little to be said on this topic, because if an applicant is refused admission that would be the end of it, still there is a decision upon the matter.[4] Plaintiff was entitled, by statute, to become a member of a County Medical Society, and it was held that admission could not be refused him, because prior to his application he had advertised in a manner contrary to the code of medical ethics ; although it was said that the society might expel any member who, being bound by such code, violated it.

<hr/>

[1] Commonwealth v. Philanthropic Society, 5 Binney, 486.

[2] Dickinson v. Chamber of Commerce, 29, Wis. 45; s. c., 9 Am. R. 544. And others were held properly expelled for gathering and forming markets before the regular time. State v. Chamber of Commerce, Wis., 1880; 10 Central L. J. 157.

[3] See note on page 596, Vol. 27 English Reports (Moak) citing Pulford v. Fire Department, 31, Mich. 458; People v. Cotton Exch., 8 Hun. 216; Becking v. Robert, 1 City, C. R. 51; State v. Cartaret, 40 N. J. L. 295.

[4] People, *rel.* Bartel v. Medical Society, 32 N. Y. 191.

If the articles of incorporation fix the nature of membership, then no other is valid; hence one admitted as a "contributing member" without authority, if afterwards expelled, can have no standing at all in court to sue for readmission.[1]

§ 15. Concerning By-Laws.— The power of making by-laws is usually quite comprehensive, yet by no means unlimited.

Dues may be fixed under by-laws, yet those dues must be in proportion to the objects for which demanded and the requirements and powers of the society; if beyond this, they are invalid.[2]

Although a member may be properly fined, say one dollar, for not joining the procession on St. Patrick's day, yet, a by-law, which deprived him of his benefits not only whilst under fine, but also for three months *after* paying the same, was held invalid.[3]

Of course it is entirely proper to withhold the benefits when intemperance was the cause of death, and to make a by-law accordingly.[4]

A case which goes to an extreme, indeed unwarrantable, extent, allowed the society to change its by-laws, so that a widow who should have received twenty-five cents per day during her widowhood, was afterward to receive that sum only until it aggregated $200, although her husband died *before* the change in the by-law was made. The court sustained the by-law on the ground that the constitution contained a clause allowing changes in the by-laws, and because the society might in times of great sickness and numerous deaths become unable to pay at all, if it were not allowed to reduce its liabilities by the change which it made.[5] It must be seen at once that the decision is not sound. Of course

[1] Diligent Fire Company v. Commonwealth, 75 Pa. St. 291.
[2] Pulford v. Detroit, F. D. 31 Mich. 458. See also Hibernia Fire Engine Co. v. Harrison, 93 Pa. St. 269, holding invalid a raise in the monthly dues from twelve and a half cents to two dollars.
[3] Cartan v. The Father Matthew U. B. S., 3 Daly (N. Y.) 20.
[4] St. Mary's B. S. v. Burford, 70 Pa. St. 321.
[5] Fugure v. Mutual Society of St. Joseph's, 46 Vermont, 362.

there was a clause in the constitution allowing changes in the by-laws, and this power is (express or implied) in every constitution; would it follow, therefore, that any society which finds that it has made improvident contracts and can not meet its death losses, can simply pass by-laws and thus reduce its debts on its policies from $1,000 to $500, or any other sum? While this may be done as to members still living, it is most certainly true that it can not be done as to the representatives of deceased members, whose rights become vested and fixed at the time of the decease. A later case [1] involving a similar question is much more satisfactory, although the decision upon this point was not necessarily called for. The case presents no arguments, and no citations of other cases, and simply states that the change in the by-laws (made somewhat as in the last case) was not intended to effect the rights of representatives of members already deceased, that is that it was not intended to be retroactive, and then states that it could *not* have been retroactive even if so intended.

A by-law existing when plaintiff joined, giving benefits to sick members, was changed so as to read that the benefit would only be payable when there were $800 on hand; it was decided that a member on joining did not become a creditor of the society, and hence that he could not recover the benefits unless there were $800 on hand.[2] (In this case the change in the by-law was made *before* the member became sick).

A by-law, involving an illegal act, is invalid. The "Good Samaritans," a benevolent society, according to their by-laws, expelled members by a sort of a mock hanging, the rope being tied about the waist. One member had aided in performing this ceremony on others, but when her own time came she refused to submit to the ordeal. Defendants insisted upon it, and were all convicted of assault and battery for doing so,[3] their by-laws being no defence to them.

[1] Gundlach v. German Mechanics Association, 4 Hun., 341.
[2] St. Patrick's Benevolent Society v. McVey, 92 Pa. St. 510.
[3] State v. Webster, 75 North Carolina, 135.

A by-law which compels members to join in a " strike'
is void, because against public policy.[1]

A corporation whose object is to " regulate the practice
of medicine" in furtherance of true science and " particularly the healing art," has no power to fix a fee bill and to
expel a member for not complying therewith; this is in
restraint of his private right ; and as the fee bill had the effect of preventing the public authorities from obtaining
medical services at prices at which they otherwise could, it
was declared void at common law.[2]

It has been said that the members of a voluntary unincorporated association are bound by its by-laws whether the
same be reasonable or not.[3] While it is, perhaps, proper to
say that a member is bound by such by-laws which were in
force when, or before, he joined (if they do not suit him
he need not join), yet, it would seem that having once
joined, and having thus obtained property rights, and ex-
pended his money thereon, that he should then be protected
against the subsequent enactment of unreasonable by-laws.
This view would seem to be in accordance with the authorities[4] which, as we have seen, protect property rights as
fully in the unincorporated societies as in the others, and it
certainly is good common sense, as a single illustration will
suffice to show.

Suppose a person joins a lodge in some benevolent order,
and for several years pays all dues and assessments, aggre-
gating a considerable amount, suppose then a small majority passes a by-law that no member should be admitted to
the meetings unless he wear a full suit of broadcloth. Evi-

[1] People, *rel.* Doyle v. N. Y. Benevolent Society of Operative Masons,
3 Hun., 361.

[2] People v. The Medical Society of County of Erie, 54 Barb., 571.

[3] See a note on page 595, Vol. 27, English Reports (Moak), citing
Elsas v. Alford, 1 City Cts. R. 123; Thompson v. Adams, 7 W. N.
(Penn.) 281; Grosvenor v. United, etc., 118 Mass. 78; Brine v. Board
of Trade, 2 Am. Law Rec. 268. These cases the writer hereof has not
been able to examine, with one exception, which (Grosvenor v. United)
related to the decision of a religious community upon the articles of its
faith.

[4] See pages 39 and following.

dently such a rule, while proper enough in some fashionable club, would be very unreasonable in a lodge composed in part of men of limited means, and it would be safe to say that no court under the canopy would allow a member to be expelled, or to be refused his rightful admission to the meetings, for a violation of such a by-law.

§ 16. **By-Law Interfering with Religious Views.**— A society incorporated for charitable and benevolent purposes can not make a by-law requiring that members attend the Catholic confessional, unless this power is reserved in the articles of incorporation or in the statutes of the State; such a by-law is not binding upon a member, though he assented to the enactment of the same.[1]

§ 17. **Sunday for Transacting Business.**— In one case the question was suggested, but not decided, whether the trial of a member could be legally held on Sunday, the court calling attention to the fact that it was not an ecclesiastical trial concerning matters of conscience, but an ordinary secular affair.[2]   But in another it was decided that not only could the trial be legally held on Sunday, but also that the notice for the same could be served on Sunday, and would be valid.[3]

§ 18. **Miscellaneous Decisions.**—Other points decided in reference to fraternities and societies, which can not well be classified in the foregoing divisions, may be grouped here.

It would seem scarcely necessary to decide that a member expelled can not recover his initiation fees, but it has been so determined.[4]

---

[1] People, *rel.* Schmitt v. St. Franciscus Benevolent Society, 24 How. Pr. 216.   See also Stewart v. Father Matthew Society, 41 Mich. 67.   If the society constitution provides for certain religious views, as Catholic Communion, then it is obligatory upon members, and is not an interference with that religious freedom which is guaranteed by the State constitution.   Hitter v. St. Aloysius Society, Kentucky, 1883, 27 Albany L. J. 431.

[2] Society for Visitation of the Sick v. Commonwealth, *rel.* Meyer, 52 Pa. St. 125.

[3] People v. Young Mens' Father Matthew Benevolent Society, 65 Barb. 357.

[4] Robinson v. Yates City Lodge, 86 Ill., 598.

Upon the question whether bequests and devises can be validly made to unincorporated voluntary associations, reference must be had to many conflicting authorities, some holding that this can not be done, and others saying that it may be, provided the association is capable of clear identification.[1]

The rule of dissolution by non-user, was applied to an unincorporated Masonic lodge, which sold off its furniture and omitted its meetings for twenty-three years. It afterwards obtained a new charter from the re-organized Grand Lodge, but it was held that it did not constitute the original subordinate lodge and was not entitled to funds in the hands of trustees remaining from the old lodge; the theory was that the old lodge had become dissolved by remaining dormant so long, and that the new lodge, though under the same name was really a different body.[2]

At the meetings of the Illinois Masonic Benevolent Society a member may vote by proxy.[3]

A member disappeared, afterward it was voted that he be regarded as dead and his policy paid; it was held that the assessment be on those who were members at date of the resolution and not those at date of the disappearance.[4]

As a matter of the utmost importance the attention of officers and members is called to the manner in which contracts, etc., should be written. If a note is written in the usual manner and signed, John Smith Treasurer of Amity Lodge, Mr. Smith could in all probability be held to pay it *himself.*

There is not space to give here the many decisions upon this topic, but the following is suggested as the safest way for drawing such papers, and all parties who may be placed in position in which they would be apt to involve themselves personally in contracts, will do well to read and " govern themselves accordingly." These suggestions ap-

---

[1] See Boone on Corporations,§§ 52, 327, 340 and cases cited.
[2] Strickland v. Prichard, 37 Vermont, 324.
[3] People v. Crossby, 69 Ill., 195.
[4] Miller v. Georgia Masonic, etc. Co., 57 Ga., 221.

ply more especially to incorporated bodies, the rules for ascertaining personal liability of members of the others given on pages 16-20.

FORM FOR A NOTE.

$100. DAVENPORT, IOWA, 188

One year after date, Amity Lodge promises to pay to the order of Wm. Jones, one hundred dollars.

(Signed). AMITY LODGE.

(By JOHN SMITH, Treasurer).

(Or by such other officer as may be authorized).

Contracts, other than notes, may be drawn in a similar manner, care being taken always to show that the promising party, and the signing party, is the association, and not the individual, who may happen to be an officer.

A few decisions appearing since the earlier pages were written, are here given, being too late for insertion elsewhere.

The widow and children under the rules of a benevolent fund, were held entitled to the fund as against the legatee.[1]

A policy taken by a brother in favor of his sister, could be changed by him to his nephew, she having died, and this could be done without consent of her representatives.[2]

The word "child" was held to include grandchild in a mutual benefit society insurance.[3]

S. was a member of the subordinate lodge, and thereby became a member of the grand lodge. The assessment of S. had been paid by the subordinate lodge to the grand lodge, but at the time of his death had not been paid by him to the subordinate lodge. The by-laws provided that "any member failing to pay his assessment within thirty days, should be suspended," and that notice should be given

---

[1] Matter of Phillips Insurance, 48 L. T. R. (N. S.) 1881; Index Reporter, May, 1883, 190.

[2] Bickerton v. Jacques, 28 Hun. 119.

[3] Winsor v. Odd Fellows Association, 13 R. I. 149.

to the grand secretary. The widow brought suit against the
grand lodge, and it was decided[1] that the mere non-payment
of the assessment did not of itself operate as suspension,
and that the act of the secretary in marking S.'s account as
"suspended" was not sufficient, as such suspension must be
made by some affirmative act of the lodge. The subordinate
lodge waived the suspension by making payment for him to
the grand lodge. The grand lodge being the only body
liable for the amount, and having received the assessment,
had thereby been paid the consideration for its obligation
to pay the beneficiary amount on the death of the member,
and was consequently ordered to pay the amount in suit.

[1] Scheu v. Grand Lodge, Ohio Division, Independent Foresters, 17 F.
R. 214.

INDEX.

BY-LAWS.
must be necessary, 53.
not contrary to common law, 53.
illustrations of valid and invalid, 61.
are unreasonable by-laws binding? 63.
or those interfering with religious views? 64.

CHARITIES.
masonic body is a public charity, 9, 10, 12.
courts take judicial notice of this, 10, 11.
it is not a public charity, 9.
Odd Fellows are not, 9.
Easton Beneficial Society is not, 11.
neither is the Ringwood Friendly Society, 11.
nor the Kennebic Masonic Relief Association, 11.
nor the Riggers and Stevedors Union, 12.
Mutual Reliance Society is not, 15.
neither is a savings bank, 15.

CHILD.
may mean grandchild, 66.

COMMERCIAL PROTECTIVE ASSOCIATION.
is not a partnership, 5.

CONTRACTS.
how to be executed, 65, 66.

CUSTOM.
cannot control the rule, 33, 34.

DISSOLUTION.
hostility among members does not suffice to cause court to decree it,
    6, 47.
of Hose Company refused so long as parties were ready to use the
    property, 6, 42.
granted on grounds of bad faith and mismanagement, 7.
or if society is merely a bubble, 8.
occurs by non-user, 65.

DIVISION.
of fund is same as in a partnership, 7.

EXPULSION.
of members, 50.
courts will give redress for improper expulsion, 50, 56.
whether society be incorporated or not, 50.
accused should have a hearing, 51, 58.
before the entire society and not a mere committee; power must be
    conferred by charter, 51.
except for certain offences, 51.
how differing from amotion, 52.
courts do not favor a too extensive power, 52.

EXPULSION—Continued.

when regularly exercised, the courts will not review the merits of the case, 54.

unless when society tribunals are insufficient, 55.

but will decide whether grounds are well taken, 55.

if long acquiesced in becomes valid, though illegal, 56.

there must be a formal act of expulsion, 58, 66, 67.

may be for causes not valid in litigation, 60.

can not be for violation of mere by-law, 60.

unless allowed by charter or statute, 60.

FAMILY.

what is meant by member of, 36.

FEES.

for initiation can not be recovered by expelled members, 64.

FORFEITURE.

not favored, 34.

how waived, 34, 35.

must be promptly asserted, 35.

and positively declared, 46, 58, 66, 67.

GOOD STANDING.

presumed, 31.

but in suing compliance with all conditions must be averred, 31.

HOSTILITY.

among members not sufficient to induce court to order dissolution, 4.

HOSE COMPANY.

is not a partnership, 6.

INSURABLE INTEREST.

the rule applies to beneficiary associations, 20.

of the wife in the life of the husband, 20.

even after divorce, 20.

the uncle has not in the nephew, 20.

nor the parent in the child, 20.

contrary view, 20.

creditor in the life of a debtor, 21.

sister in the life of a brother, 21.

a woman in the life of her betrothed, 21.

a person in the life of a business partner, 21.

how to determine this question, 22.

JURISDICTION.

relation of society tribunals to the courts of the State, 38.

how and when the courts have jurisdiction, 39, 40.

they will protect the rights of members, 39.

REINSTATEMENT.
can not be asked after damages recovered for expulsion, 56.

RELIGIOUS ASSOCIATIONS.
not included in this book, 2.

RELIGIOUS VIEWS.
affected by by-laws, 64.

"RELIEF FUND."
cases, 45.

RULES.
what is meant by this term, 33.
may be waived by contract, 35.
members must know them, and are bound by them, 32, 33.

SLANDER AND LIBEL.
society communications are privileged, 47.

SUICIDE.
does not invalidate policy unless so stipulated, 36.

SUNDAY.
for transacting business, 64.

TAXATION.
the society property is not subject to taxation, 9, 10.
contrary view, 9.

VOTE.
may be by proxy, 65.

WIDOW.
who is, 37.

WILL.
when designation in will controls the policy, 28.
when it does not, 26, 28, 29.

www.ingramcontent.com/pod-product-compliance
Lightning Source LLC
Chambersburg PA
CBHW020252290326
41930CB00039B/1039